Ruthie O. Gran'

I Thought I Was The Crazy One

201 Ways To Identify and Deal With Toxic Personalities

At this point in my life I want to live as if only love matters; as if the search to live honestly is all that anyone needs-Tracy Chapman

PERSONHOOD PRESS
"Books for all that you are!"
www.personhoodpress.com
personhoodpress@att.net
800-662-9662

I Thought I Was The Crazy One

PERSONHOOD PRESS
P. O. Box 1185 Torrance, California 90505

I Thought I Was the Crazy One is intended to be educational and in no way a substitute for specific advice from a physician or mental health expert. If you or someone you know are feeling unstable, seek professional help at once. The author and publisher expressly disclaim responsibility for any negative effects directly or indirectly attributable to the use or application of any information contained in this book.

PRAISE FOR
I Thought I Was the Crazy One

"Most of us don't pay attention to clues that could tell us we are with a potential Jack the Ripper or Lizzy Borden. "I Thought I Was the Crazy One" provides clues to prevent one from overlooking the obvious. All too often we sweep the evidence under the carpet." - *ALYCE LaVIOLETE, M.S., MFCC, Author and founder of ALTERNATIVES TO VIOLENCE*

"I find myself reading excerpts to friends who are going through crises in their relationships. It's like my own personal Bible on relationships." - *CARRIE SEE, Photographer, Los Angeles.*

"This book is not just for women. Men will see themselves in it. Those who are enlightened will be moved by it." -*VALERIE ROBESON, BEVERLY HILLS*

PRAISE FOR
I Thought I Was The Crazy One

"The author deals with a heavy topic in a lighthearted, entertaining way and an easy to read format. She also dispels stereotypes and addresses important contemporary relationship issues." *-FRAN CLOSE, founder, AMERICAN BUSINESS WOMEN INTERNATIONAL*

WARNING: I Thought I Was The Crazy One is a thought-provoking book. The author translates difficult concepts succinctly. Her humor and inner strength guide the reader, male or female, to 'pragmatic insights'." *-MARJI MARTIN, President, WOMEN'S ENTERTAINMENT NETWORK*

"A timeless book whose time has finally come!" – *JEANNIE MORGAN CHRISTOPHER, DALLAS, TEXAS*

"This book afforded me a new awareness of women and a better understanding of myself as a man." - **ROBERT ISMIRNOFF, L.A. ACCOUNTANT**

I Thought I Was The Crazy One

Ruthie O. Grant

For speaking engagements
contact the author at:
818-203-9929
email: docruth1@aol.com
www.ithoughtiwasthecrazyone.com

COMING SOON by The Author:

"The Wings of Words"

"Circumstantial Evidence"

"The Vrill Society"

DEDICATED TO:

The Memory of my Mother,
LOUELLA RICHARD,
who deserved so much more
and didn't even know it;

The Memory of my Teacher,
MRS. E. E. O'BANION,
who first taught me to value
my intellect and my self; and,

My Bright, discerning Daughter,
Crystal, who is much wiser than I was
at her age.

ACKNOWLEDGMENTS

Cover painting by LaMarche.

Author's Photo by Demayo.

Design and layout of cover by Pierre-Martin Drolet.

Thanks to my daughter, Crystal, for her emotional support, insightful suggestions, and input.

Special thanks to RON KRAFKA for his generous support and assistance.

Thanks to my ex-husband, HORACE, for the lessons in adversity placed in my path. I learned to succeed because of them.

FOREWORD

This book provides ways to identify potentially toxic personalities along with survival skills to deal with those who drive everyone around them crazy by "demanding much, giving little, and treating others shabbily." Everyone will exhibit some of the warning signs; however, beware of those who possess an overwhelming percentage of them. Toxic personalities rarely, if ever, accept blame or responsibility and operate from the primitive parts of their brains, which means that they lack compassion, empathy or insight into the consequences of their behavior. Change is difficult for them, which forces you to confront their unresolved issues over, and over, and over again while they lead you to believe that you are the crazy one.

There is no known cause or cure for toxic personalities. They tend to actively resist or avoid treatment. As a result, this book was designed to help those who live, work or associate with personality disorders who "perceive themselves as superior beings in a hostile, dog-eat-dog world in which others are competitors for power and resources (Hare 195)." Their game is winning at all costs. Ultimately, one has to decide if the price one is asked to pay is worth the cost of remaining with such a person -Ruthie O. Grant

TABLE OF CONTENTS

PART I

PART II

Table of Contents
(Continued)

PART III

Table of Contents
(Continued)

A Note From The Author

In the tradition of Vietnamese author, Thich Nhat Hahn, this material is not set forth as "absolute truths," but rather, as "guiding principles" to help one identify toxic personalities, and then determine, through the information provided, if one can find a way to co-exist with that person without being driven crazy; if it is time to seek professional help; or, if it is in the best interest of both parties to dissolve the relationship. In the latter situation, this book provides help in overcoming the emotional damage done to one's self image and self esteem by toxic personalities.

The author respects the timeless and ageless universality of truth and presents it without attachment to doctrines, individuals, or belief systems. Overall, the goal is to remind readers that "you are the one you are looking for" (Audre Lourde) and that "to love oneself is the beginning of a life long romance" (Oscar Wilde). The book is not intended as a substitute for professional help or intervention. For additional resources, a list of reference materials is provided.

A great deal of the research in Part II and III is simplified, condensed, excerpted, and/or adapted from the works of authors, philosophers, metaphysicians and experts who came before me. I wish to acknowledge them and honor the path they have laid out for others to follow, which prevents one from having to reinvent the wheel.

My goal was to come up with a single, concise little book that contains pearls of wisdom from many sources that go right to the heart of relationship and self esteem issues addressed in this book.

In Part III, I am indebted to the following authors: Lorna S. Benjamin, Catherine Cardinal, Barbara De'Angelis, Donald G. Dutton, Dr. Riane Eisler, Thich Nhat Hanh, Gina O'Connell Higgins, Carolyn Heilbrun, L. Ron Hubbard, Alyce LaViolette, Jan Kennedy, Dr. Victoria Lee, Dr. Gregory W. Lester, Barry Long, Maya Pines, Linda Sanford & Mary E. Donovan, Dr. Len Sperry, Neale Donald Walsh, and Marianne Williamson.

In Part I and Part II, I am indebted to a long list of authors whose names are acknowledged on each page after their quotes.   - Ruthie O. Grant

PREFACE

Our culture and society can define us, our expectations, dreams, and to some degree, our realities. For many, that may mean a life characterized by adaptation. Most people learn more about the needs of others than they do about their own needs. Many believe their value is defined by their attachment to a man or a woman.

For some, being single is worse than living with an emotionally or physically violent person. The critical point is to believe that we are as important to ourselves as we make our significant others important to us. We need to look to see who fits for us. Compatibility of values is a key issue. If you understand your own "bottom line" you will be able to discern whether or not this person shares them - not just in word but in action. Men or women who may be dangerous to your self-image often let you know by "advising," "parenting," "pouting," or "putting down." Others "spray" their territory, marking their property -- that property may be you.

Most of us don't pay attention to the clues that could tell us we are with a potential Jack the Ripper, or Lizzy Borden. This book provides clues to prevent one from overlooking the obvious. All too often we sweep the evidence under the carpet. First things first--pay attention to the evidence. It is important to Beware of a Person Who ... leads but will not follow; reacts at a level where you begin to alter your behavior because of an anticipated over-reaction; and, is rigid and inflexible when faced with change. If a relationship is a good one, we can be proud of the person we are in that relationship with.

-ALYCE LaVIOLETTE, M.S., MFCC,
Founder of ALTERNATIVES TO VIOLENCE

INTRODUCTION

"I Thought I Was The Crazy One" contains, on each page, one clear warning of problems that might develop should you ignore these warnings. Expect to grow if you heed them. Beware of ignoring them: You could become a statistic.

This is a book full of information you need to live a positive, productive life, and to have a healthy relationship with the most important person in your life: yourself. I'm proud to be associated with this book.

No one needs permission to have rights and responsibilities.A healthy relationship includes respect for individuals and their differences.

The "Theater of Hope For Abused Women" has a brochure that lists "Your Rights and Responsibilities." They include: "to feel safe and live without fear, especially in your own home; to say no without feeling guilty and selfish; to establish goals and to work toward attaining those goals; to express your feelings and the right to choose not to; to privacy; to socialize with others; to change yourself; to ask for help; not to be perfect."

-MARJI MARTIN, President
WOMEN'S ENTERTAINMENT NETWORK

Beware of a Person Who ...

PART I

201 WAYS TO IDENTIFY AND DEAL WITH TOXIC PERSONALITIES

He will choose you, disarm you with his words, and control you with his presence. He will delight you with his wit and his plans. He will show you a good time, but you will always get the bill. He will smile and deceive you, and he will scare you with his eyes. And when he is through with you, and he will be through with you, he will desert you and take with him your innocence and your pride. You will be left much sadder but not a lot wiser, and for a long time you will wonder what happened and what you did wrong. And if another of his kind comes knocking at your door, will you open it?

-Excerpted from an essay signed "A Psychopath in Prison"
-From "Without Conscience" by Robert D. Hare, PhD

1

Beware of a Person Who ...

is a Tinman or Tinwoman (unfaithful heartbreakers) with holes in their hearts so big no one man or woman can ever fill them up. Have the foresight and fortitude to kick the Tinman or Tinwoman habit.

[Note: The following also applies to women] "Some men need the security of a steady relationship to feel confident enough to chase women. That's why you may not realize he's a lady's man at first: until he is sure he has you hooked, and knows his bait works, he is too insecure to troll for other romantic prey." -Carol Lieberman, M.D. & Lisa Cool

Beware of a Person Who ...

amputates sexuality from a meaningful act of love. Since he or she cannot connect common sense with the seat of passion, this type will use sex as a substitute for emotional closeness.

"Controlling and/or abusive men or women "confuse sexuality with intimacy and offer their partners sex rather than emotional closeness." -Hawker & Bicehouse

Tom Stoppard in "The Real Thing" defined love as knowing and being known. In ancient Greece knowing was used for making love, or carnal knowledge - knowledge of the self -- the mask slipped from the face. Every other version of the self is an offer to the public." -Arianna Huffington

Beware of a Person Who ...

finds fault in others without examining his or her own shortcomings. A wise person will strive not to marry weaknesses, nor make lovers of them, but will work hard at overcoming his or her own faults. Anyone overly critical of others is obviously not sure of self.

"Men [and women] will preserve the errors of their childhood, of their country, and of their age long after having recognized all the truths needed to destroy them." -Marquis de Condorat

"When a man [or woman] spends his/her time giving his/her wife/husband criticism and advice instead of compliments, he/she forgets that it was not his/her good judgment, but his/her charming manners, that won his/her heart."-Helen Rowland

Beware of a Person Who ...

is attracted to strong women or men only to rob them of their power. As a child, an adult probably made this type feel powerless. Now someone has to pay for the pain. That someone is you. An abusive person will beat you down emotionally before beating you up physically. Leave once the verbal abuse begins. This will help the abuser realize that there are consequences for bad behavior.

"Power abdicates only under the stress of counter power."
-Martin Buber

Beware of a Person Who ...

has serious character deficits (i.e. dishonesty, laziness, insensitivity, etc). It is commonly known that those with character disorders make every one else miserable. Unless this person is actively working on changing bad character traits, you are in for a lifetime of misery. Leave this one to wallow in dysfunction alone.

"When those with character disorders are in conflict with the world they automatically assume the world is at fault ... [and are] impossible to work with because they don't see themselves as the source of their problems [and] fail to recognize the necessity for self examination."   -M. Scott Peck

Beware of a Person Who ...

thinks that an individual's worth is measured primarily through material means without including the weight of moral values. Don't expect substance from a superficial person, nor sensitivity from someone who places little or no value on ethical or moral issues.

"Knowledge is, indeed, that which, next to virtue, truly and essentially raises one man/woman above another" -- not material possessions. -Joseph Addison

Materialists and madmen never have doubts." - 4th Earl of Chesterfield

Beware of a
Person Who ...

makes a career out of rescuing women or men with promises and lies that he/she cannot possibly live up to. This type is a Wizard of Fraud, who cannot even save him/herself, let alone anyone else. Those on a mission to save the world must first make sure that they've saved themselves.

"Why wait for a Wizard to lift you above the bleak circumstances of your life, or painful memories, when you can attack these problems on your own?"   -Carole Lieberman, M.D. & Lisa Cool

"Relationships riddled with lies leave us wondering ... why we gave our power and time to the liar rather than to our own best interests." -Dory Hollander, PhD

Beware of a Person Who ...

acts out of compulsion as opposed to reason. This person will lack discipline and find it difficult, if not impossible, to delay gratification. So, unless you want to live with a perpetual two year old, who demands that his/her needs be met NOW, pass on this one.

"To have discipline, we must be totally dedicated to truth [and] always hold truth ... to be more important, more vital to our self interest, than our comfort ... Mental health is an ongoing process of dedication to reality at all costs." -M. Scott Peck

Beware of a Person Who ...

majors in minor matters. Greatness rarely resides in small minds. Such a person will consider him/herself a visionary when, in reality, she/he is a mere dreamer caught in trivial pursuit of petty problems while blind to the big picture.

"One might call habit a moral friction: something that prevents the mind from gliding over things, but connects it with them and makes it hard for it to free itself from them." -G.C. Lichtenberg

"Every disorder of the soul is its own punishment."- Saint Augustine

Beware of a Person Who ...

is a tyrant and proud to carry the title.

"Tyrants have not yet discovered any chains that can fetter the mind." -Charles Caleb Colton

"Any excuse will serve a tyrant." -Aesop

"Do not put such unlimited power into the hands of the husbands. Remember, all men would be tyrants if they could." -Abigail Smith Adams

Beware of a Person Who ...

has no close friends and tries to build an entire world around you. That may be fine for a Marvin Gaye song ("If I Could Build My Whole World Around You"), but we all need outside associations. Stay in touch with old friends and keep all exits open.

"A man and a woman make far better friendships than can exist between two of the same sex - but then with the condition that they never have made or are to make love to each other." -Lord Byron

"Always keep some cab fare tucked in your bosom...'cause you never know what the evening is going to bring." - Mother Love

Beware of a Person Who ...

idealizes his or her parents. Adults who view their parents as perfect or ideal tend to be in denial or afraid that they will never measure up. Individuation requires separation from parents; accepting that they have faults like everyone else, and that it is okay to surpass our parents' achievements and learn from their mistakes.

"A child who is not loved by his/her parents will always assume himself or herself to be unlovable rather than see the parents as deficient in their capacity to love." -M. Scott Peck

Beware of a
Person Who ...

*is a "Mama's Boy" or a "Daddy's Girl."
No matter how old he or she
becomes, operating independently will
be a challenge. Moreover, this person
might take his or her co-dependence
issues out on you.*

"Discourage over dependency. If he/she is ever to grow up and become a prince/princess, your lover has to learn how to make a healthy separation from [parents] - or you." - Carole Lieberman, M.D. & Lisa Cool

Beware of a Person Who ...

lives for happy hour or to party on weekends. This type of superficiality can indicate an addictive compulsive personality in need of constant excitement. Why would you want to be with someone who is unable to enjoy the solitude of his or her own company?

"To be a slave to pleasure is the life of a harlot, not of a man." -Anacreon

15

Beware of a
Person Who ...

thinks nothing of putting unreasonable demands upon others without a hint of gratitude. Not only will this person expect you to cater to his or her wishes, but will become indignant should you refuse. Unless you enjoy serving an ingrate, you might want to stay clear of this one.

"Good fellowship and friendship are lasting, rational and manly pleasures." -William Wycherley

Beware of a
Person Who ...

is over 40 and has never been engaged, married, or involved in a serious, long term relationship. This type of person may be: afraid of, or avoiding commitment; have unrealistic expectations; incredibly selfish or self-centered; unfaithful; set in his or her ways; or, bisexual and looking for someone to bear a child. Take this one on only if you are desperate or enjoy challenges.

"Selfish persons are incapable of loving others, but they are not capable of loving themselves either." -Erich Fromm

Beware of a
Person Who ...

insults, talks down to, belittles, or is discourteous to those from lower socio-economic levels, or different ethnic backgrounds. Avoid small minded, insecure, and unenlightened individuals.

"The chief cause of human error is to be found in prejudices picked up in childhood." -Rene Descartes

"I can't stand a naked light bulb, any more than I can a rude remark or a vulgar action." -Tennessee Williams

Beware of a Person Who ...

shows no compassion for the plight of those in need. Regard for the welfare of others is a pretty good indicator of how this person will respond to your needs once the honeymoon's over.

"Man should not consider his material possessions his own, but as common to all, so as to share them without hesitation when others are in need." -Saint Thomas Aquinas

"Giving and service are the path back to God."- Arianna Huffington

19

Beware of a
Person Who ...

is chintzy, grudging, or miserly with when it comes to spending; especially on you. Stinginess does not respect boundaries. It reaches into all areas, limiting access to the finer things in life.

"While you have a thing it can be taken from you ... but when you give it, you have given it. No robber can take it from you. It is yours then forever when you have given it. It will be yours always. That is to give." -James Joyce

"It is rare indeed that people give. Most people guard and keep; they suppose that it is they themselves and what they identify with themselves that they are guarding and keeping, whereas they are actually guarding and keeping their system of reality and what they assume themselves to be." -James Baldwin

Beware of a Person Who ...

mistreats you in private, yet in public, acts as if you hung the moon, while pretending to be your guardian angel. Such a person will use favorable public opinion to convince you that if you only acted right, he or she wouldn't have to behave so badly because it's really your fault.

"In doing good avoid fame. In doing bad, avoid disgrace. Pursue a middle course as your principle." Chauang-Tzu

"Fidelity to conscience is inconsistent with retiring modesty. If it be so, let the modesty succumb. It can be only a false modesty which can be thus endangered." -Harriet Martineau

Beware of a
Person Who ...

on the first date, invites you to an expensive restaurant, waits until the bill arrives, then tells you it's a Dutch Date. That is as bad as being invited to a birthday dinner without the host telling you in advance that you're expected to pay for your own meal.

"Smart men/women know that God created dating so that a man/woman could discover the bad news about" the other before getting involved, not after. -Carter & Sokal

Beware of a Person Who ...

drinks in excess. Marguerite Duras says that "Alcohol always ends in despair ... It doesn't console, it doesn't fill up anyone's psychological gaps, all it replaces is the lack of God. It doesn't comfort man."

"The drunken man is a living corpse." -St. John Chrysostom

"If he has an active addiction, refuse to be an accomplice in it .. He isn't free to give his heart to you ... [and could] hate you for tolerating his toxic habit." -Carole Lieberman, M.D. & Lisa Cool

23

Beware of a Person Who ...

is a coward. The growth potential in your relationship will be limited by this person's fears and crippled by phobias.

"Perfect courage is to do without witnesses what one would be capable of doing with the world looking on." -Francois, Duc de la Rochefoucauld

"Fear is stronger than arms." -Aechylus

"To see what is right and not to do it is cowardice." - Confucius

"Courage is the knowledge of knowing what is not to be feared." -Pericles

Beware of a Person Who ...

puts a premium on laughter, or complains that you laugh too loud. This one just might graduate to limiting the dimensions of joy.

"Laughter is God's therapy -- in order that we might understand that at the heart of our mortal existence there lies a mystery at once unnaturally beautiful and hilariously funny." -Arianna Huffington

"There exists a kind of laughter which is worthy to be ranked with the higher lyric emotions ..." -Nikolai Vasilyevich Gogol

"To jealousy, nothing is more frightful than laughter." -Francoise Sagan

"Laughter ... extends a hand into the waters of pain but remains standing on firm ground." -Hugh & Gayle Prather

Beware of a Person Who ...

has a pattern of being long suffering, pretentious or uneasy in the presence of important or influential people that you know, while refusing to allow you to mingle alone. This type is not likely to let you go anywhere in life unless it's all about him or her.

"The mark of the man of the world is absence of pretension." -Ralph Waldo Emerson

"An oppressed people are authorized whenever they can to rise and break their fetters." - Henry Clay

Beware of a Person Who ...

complains about, or refuses to wear a condom. Value your life too much to give in to lame arguments on this issue. You don't know how many people he or she has had unprotected sex with. No condom -- no condiments.

"You are wiser than you think." -Anonymous

"Sex is as important as eating or drinking and we ought to allow the one appetite to be satisfied with as little false modesty as the other." -Marquis de Sade

"A man's ease in taking indecent liberties with his identity, occupation, finances, sexual history, or whatever, makes it a challenge for a woman to differentiate fact from fiction; prince from frog." -Dory Hollander, PhD

Beware of a
Person Who ...

does not have an innate sense of propriety. Do you really want to be with a person who relies on someone else's idea of what is proper under questionable circumstances? Find a person who can make his or her own decisions.

"In all of life, never, ever, ever, fail to do something simply because it might violate someone else's standards of propriety." -Neale Donald Walsch

Beware of a Person Who ...

does not say: "please," "thank you," or "pardon me." Chances are, if a person takes simple pleasantries for granted he or she will also take you for granted.

"Excellent things are rare." -Plato

"A thought once awakened does not slumber." -Carlyle

Beware of a
Person Who ...

establishes his or her own dress code for you, or dictates what you should wear in public. Who appointed this one fashion police or designer of the week?

"Work on your appearance. Another responsibility you have is to be the best-looking that you can be, given what you came with." -K Callan

"Why should I limit myself just because people won't accept the fact that I can do something else?" -Dolly Parton

"Resolve to be thyself; and know, that he who finds himself loses his misery." -Arnold

Beware of a
Person Who ...

has no concept of preventative problem solving skills. You'll find this person stranded on the side of the road in the heat of summer, or skating on thin ice in winter because he or she avoided regular or routine car maintenance.

"If you are not part of the solution, then you are part of the problem." -Eldridge Cleaver

Beware of a Person Who ...

in the presence of a wisdom holder, is not smart enough to sit quietly, listen, and learn. Those who demean, criticize, or challenge the wise are fools. What will that make the two of you?

"Cleverness is not wisdom." –Euripides

"Wisdom is knowledge applied." -Neale Donald Walsch

Beware of a Person Who ...

is rude to waiters or waitresses. Those who serve the food that nourishes and sustains life should be treated with the highest esteem and respect. What's to stop this one from treating you with the same disrespect in your kitchen?

"The evolution of a society is measured by how well it treats the least among its members." -Neale Donald Walsch

Beware of a
Person Who ...

is unaware that receptionists and secretaries can influence the decisions of their bosses by acting as guardians to the gates of opportunity. Clearly this one doesn't know that secretaries are important gatekeepers and can accidentally-on-purpose fail to put a call through or shut the door of opportunity in ones face.

"Whatever debases the intelligence degrades the entire human being."-Simone Weil

*"Cruelty is a mystery, and the waste of pain."
-Annie Dillard*

Beware of a
Person Who ...

is too lazy to learn a foreign language, yet criticizes the English of foreigners working hard to learn a second language. This one needs to walk a mile in the other person's shoes.

"Judge halfheartedly." -Hugh and Gayle Prather

"What is the point of being here if you're not involved? To me, you must keep working. When I still have curiosity and energy and want to do things, that tells me I'm alive." - Lauren Bacall at age 72

Beware of a
Person Who ...

does not value travel to foreign lands or exposure to different cultures. That's not the only thing this type will be closed to. Eventually you'll end up weary from keeping count of the long list of things he or she simply cannot stomach -- yourself included.

"My favorite thing is to go where I've never been." - Diane Arbus

"A journey is like marriage. The certain way to be wrong is to think you control it." -John Steinbeck

Beware of a Person Who ...

only eats meat and potatoes. Don't expect intellectual acrobatics out of a constipated mind. Since we are what we eat, a conscious being will adhere to healthy dietary habits.

"The preservation of health is a duty. Few seem conscious that there is such a thing as physical morality." -Herbert Spencer

"Health is a state of complete physical, mental and social well-being, and not merely the absence of disease or infirmity." -Constitution. The World Health Organization

Beware of a Person Who ...

confuses a vacation with staying home from work and catching up on sleep, or a trip to Blockbuster Video; and, is always in a hurry to get home and do nothing.

"For my part, I travel not to go anywhere, but to go. I travel for travel's sake. The great affair is to move; to feel the needs and hitches of our life." - *Robert Louis Stevenson*

"The main dangers in life are the people who want to change everything ... or nothing." -*Lady Astor*

Beware of a Person Who ...

does not appreciate the beauty of snow capped mountains; starry nights; or, the subtle phases of the moon; wouldn't dream of stopping to watch the sun set at sea; and, can't even comprehend getting up at dawn to greet the rising of the sun. Do not expect those who fail to appreciate the beauty of nature, to appreciate your real beauty either.

"Millions dream of immortality who do not know what to do with themselves on a rainy Sunday afternoon."
-Susan Ertz

Beware of a Person Who ...

places rules over safety. Under difficult or challenging circumstances, he or she will be unable to make practical, sensible, or common sense decisions. Rule followers stamp out their own freedom of choice.

"The young man knows the rules, but the old man knows the exceptions." -Oliver Wendell Holmes

"There is a time to let go of rules altogether." -Gavin de Becker

Beware of a Person Who ...

thinks it is immasculine or too sentimental to fully feel the emotion of a moment that calls for a little tenderness and tears. This type may be insecure about his sexual identity.

*"Masculinity can only be experienced, achieved, recognized, and embodied in opposition to femininity."
-Andrea Dworkin*

"Masculinity is not something given to you, but something you gain. And you gain it by winning small battles with honor." -Norman Mailer

"A woman simply is, but a man must become. Masculinity is risky and elusive." - Camille Pagila

Beware of a Person Who ...

is neurotic. M. Scott Peck defines a neurosis as "a disorder of responsibility in relating to problems, people or situations." Since association breeds assimilation, if you stay with such a person, his/her neurosis is likely to rub off on you.

"When neurotics are in conflict with the world they automatically assume that they are at fault... Distinguishing what we are and what we are not responsible for in this life is one of the greatest problems of human existence." -M. Scott Peck

Beware of a Person Who ...

uses the expression "I love you," as a substitute for actually loving you. With those who really love you, their actions will match their words.

"Love that seeks aught but the disclosure of its own mystery is not love but a net cast forth and only the unprofitable is caught." -Kahlil Gibran

"Love can all but raise the dead." -Emily Dickinson

"Love and a cough cannot be concealed. Even a small cough. Even a small love." -Ann Sexton

Beware of a
Person Who ...

formulates an opinion about others based on hearsay or second hand information; or, shifts blame from self on to innocent others.

"The single greatest power in the world today is the power to change ... The most recklessly irresponsible thing we can do in the future would be to go on exactly as we have in the past." -Karl W. Deutsch

"To accuse others of one's own misfortunes is a sign of want of education; to accuse oneself shows that one's education has begun; to accuse neither oneself nor others shows that one's education is complete." -Epictetus

"The inability to experience the suffering of another as one's own is what allows such suffering to continue." -Neale Donald Walsch

Beware of a
Person Who ...

is a card carrying pessimist. What could you possibly want with a wet noodle who feels entitled to rain on your parade?

"Pessimism is an important predictor of problems (just as optimism is an important predictor of success)." - Gavin de Becker

Beware of a Person Who ...

takes offense easily. King Solomon reveals that "the taking of offense is in the heart of the stupid ones."

"Give the gift of an innocent vision to everyone you see."
-Hugh and Gayle Prather

"If you come across any special trait of meanness or stupidity ... you must be careful not to let it annoy or distress you, but to look upon it merely as an addition to your knowledge - a fact to be considered in studying the character of humanity." -Schopenhauer

Beware of a Person Who ...

is judgmental. Unless this person has been officially elected to the position of Judge, he or she has no legitimate claim to the rights of that office.

No man can judge another, because no man knows himself."
-Sir Thomas Browne

"The man of belief is necessarily a dependent man .. he does not belong to himself, but to the author of the idea he believes." -Friedrich Nietzsche

Beware of a Person Who ...

knows everything. A closed mind is not open to receiving anything new and very little worth hearing ever comes out either.

"Your treasured opinions never made anyone happy." -Hugh and Gayle Prather

"Only the educated are free." -Epictetus

"He who neglects learning ... loses the past and is dead for the future." -Euripides

Beware of a Person Who ...

is suspicious without just cause. Perhaps he or she is the one who shouldn't be trusted?

"The suspicious mind believes more than it doubts. It believes in a formidable and ineradicable evil lurking in every person." -Eric Hoffer

"Suspicion is not less an enemy to virtue than to happiness; he that is already corrupt is naturally suspicious, and he that becomes suspicious will quickly be corrupt." -Joseph Addison

"We are paid for our suspicions by finding what we suspected." -Henry David Thoreau

Beware of a Person Who ...

falsely accuses you of infidelity. Chances are, this person is the one who is unfaithful and feels an extraordinary sense of entitlement to cheat on you.

"If you love another, you will not do anything that you believe could or would hurt that person." - Neale Donald Walsch

"The voice of honest indignation is the voice of God." -William Blake

"Dare to be wise." -Horace

Beware of a Person Who ...

is on the opposite end of your biological sleep clock. When the other person is asleep, _you'll_ be awake, wanting to talk, or when you're sleepy, this person will feel amorous, and want you to wake up and make love.

"Betrayal of yourself in order not to betray another is betrayal nonetheless. It is the highest betrayal." - Neale Donald Walsch

"The secrets of life are not shown except to sympathy and likeness." -Emerson

Beware of a
Person Who ...

interrogates. Keep your own counsel and answer a question that invades your privacy or human rights with another question.

"Those who deny freedom to others deserve it not for themselves, and under a just God, cannot long retain it." -Abraham Lincoln

Beware of a
Person Who ...

intimidates. Most are bullies with
chips on their shoulders designed to
make the meek cower or cater to
them. When confronted by a
courageous or superior rival, they will
back down to avoid being conquered
because it's all about winning with
them.

*"It's okay to be angry - as long as you use the anger
as a healthy force for change." -Carole Lieberman,
M.D. & Lisa Cool*

"Anger is fear announced." -Neale Donald Walsch

Beware of a Person Who ...

knowingly commits a crime and expects you to stand by him while he does the time.

"When desperadoes ride off into the sunset, they ride off alone." -Carter & Sokol

"Sometimes the best way to love someone, and the most help you can give, is to leave them alone or empower them to help themselves." -Neale Donald Walsch

Beware of a Person Who ...

is paranoid. Paranoid individuals blame anything that goes wrong on others because they believe that people are out to get them. Gavin De Becker, in "The Gift of Fear" refers to this type of person as a "Scriptwriter."

"The "Scriptwriter" gives no credit when people are helpful and this causes alienation. [He is] not receptive to suggestions because he takes them as affronts or criticisms of his way of doing things." - Gavin De Becker

Beware of a
Person Who ...

needs you at his or her constant beck and call, then makes you feel guilty when you're not readily available. Eventually this individual will move to requiring relinquishment of your autonomy and individuality.

"If your man/woman didn't think you'd expect something in return -- like a commitment - he/she'd wear you around his/her neck like a pacifier, and comfort him/herself with you all day long." -Carole Lieberman, M.D. & Lisa Cool

"Needing someone is the fastest way to kill a relationship." -Neale Donald Walsch

Beware of a Person Who ...

is a guilt catcher. He or she was well trained at home to put the wishes and demands of parents and siblings before the well being of his/her self or mate. This one will have a hard time learning (if ever) to switch gears and place the needs of self or mate first.

"Men willingly believe what they wish." -Caius Julius Caesar

Beware of a Person Who ...

is a master controller with little or no self control. This type will be busy trying to control you while unaware that the only behavior he or she has any control over is his or her own.

A man/woman with control issues is "blind to the effects of his/her controlling behavior." -Hawker & Bicehouse

"Seek not to make of your love a glue that binds, but rather a magnet that first attracts, then turns around and repels, least those who are attracted begin to believe that they must stick to you to survive." -Neale Donald Walsch

Beware of a Person Who ...

allows himself or herself to be controlled. This poor person will look to you as a personal guide the way the Tinman, Scarecrow, and The Lion looked to Dorothy to lead them to the Wizard of Oz. Encourage such a person to get a Guru.

"As long as you can find someone else to blame for anything you are doing, you cannot be held accountable or responsible for your growth or the lack of it." - Sun Bear

Beware of a Person Who ...

is inflexible in small matters. This individual won't be able to budge on big issues either and that could cost you dearly in the long run. Enroll this one in a yoga class to learn how to bend. Hopefully, he/she won't break.

"A free society cherishes non-conformity." -Henry Steele Commanger

Beware of a Person Who ...

is a cheap imitation of a show piece. Should you decide to settle for a shiny, inexpensive piece of hematite, a million years short of becoming a diamond, then only heaven can help you as you wait on the conversion. Why not go for the real thing?

"Truth, like light, blinds. Falsehood, on the contrary, is a beautiful twilight that enhances every object." - Albert Camus

Beware of a
Person Who ...

rearranges reality to be right. Even if this person is as wrong as two left feet, shifting blame is the name of the game because this type cannot take responsibility for any wrong doing.

"Denial and blame are part of all abusive relationships. Abusers tend to put responsibility for their actions on people and situations around them."
-Hawker & Bicehouse

Beware of a
Person Who ...

creates an altered version of the truth, then convinces you that you heard wrong; or, deliberately manipulates the situation to make you wonder if your mind is playing tricks on you.

"Abusive men have perceptual problems. Their interpretation of an incident does not have to make sense to anyone else." -Alyce LaViolette

Beware of a Person Who ...

avoids books, tapes or films that foster personal growth. You'll end up stuck with a petrified mind in a rigid body mired in his animal instincts, unable to reach a higher level of consciousness.

"I have taken all knowledge to be my province."
-Roger Bacon

Beware of a Person Who ...

undermines your belief in your abilities in order to steer you away from the path leading to your dreams. Careful: those lead astray rarely find their way back to the high road.

> "Love seeketh not Itself to please,
> Nor for itself hath any care,
> But for another gives its ease,
> And builds a Heaven in Hell's despair."
> -William Blake

Beware of a Person Who ...

does not rejoice in your successes or accomplishments. Stop to read the warning signs. Chances are he or she is jealous of the attention you get from others and will find subtle ways to block your achievements.

"The worst part of success is to try finding someone who is happy for you." –Bette Midler

Beware of a Person Who ...

criticizes or finds fault with your ideas and suggestions without coming up with anything better to replace them with.

"Think wrongly, if you please, but in all cases think for yourself." -Doris Lessin

"Cynicism is cheap -- you can buy it at any Monoprix store -- it's built into all poor-quality goods." - Graham Greene

Beware of a Person Who ...

feels an "extraordinary sense of entitlement." This personality type will place unreasonable demands that could require sacrifice of your "self" or your soul.

"Some of these persistent people suffer from delusions ... a false belief that cannot be shaken even in the face of compelling contrary evidence." -Gavin De Becker

"For to sin, indeed is human, but to persevere in sin is not human but altogether Satanic." -St. John Chrysostom

Beware of a Person Who ...

doesn't support your goals, plans, or dreams; "accidentally-on-purpose" sabotages your success; then, offers lame excuses for his/her behavior.

"Fight hesitantly. Judge halfheartedly. Be happy unnecessarily. Say what is easily forgotten. Do what is easily overlooked. Think what is everlasting." - Hugh and Gayle Prather

"What you are speaks so loud I cannot hear you." - Anonymous

Beware of a
Person Who ...

embarrasses you in public by arguing loudly over an insignificant issue. Use the one strike rule here.

"Don't compromise yourself.   You are all that you've got."   -Janis Joplin

Beware of a Person Who ...

invariably takes the other person's side in a disagreement that involves you, even when that person is clearly in the wrong. Maybe this person never heard of loyalty, but such behavior should provide a clue to what he or she really thinks of you. Refuse to have such a person in your life.

"Elegance is refusal." -Coco Chanel

Beware of a Person Who ...

allows his/her parents to demean, disrespect or insult you without speaking up in your defense (while in your presence). It does not count if you are told that the parents were straightened out after you left.

The key to "possessing the secret of joy is resistance." -Alice Walker

Beware of a
Person Who ...

says "Trust me." Usually this can be interpreted to mean that such a person wants you to sit back and let him or her take control of your life, whether you like it or not.

"When one does not know how to convince, one oppresses; in all power relations among governors and governed, as ability declines, usurpation increases." - Madame de Stael

Beware of a Person Who ...

makes promises he or she has no intention of keeping or, breaks promises without blinking an eye. He or she will be a source of constant disappointment. Do you really want to be bothered with someone you can't count on?

"Without knowing the force of words it is impossible to know men." -Confucius

"It is flattering some people to endure them." -Marquess of Halifax

Beware of a Person Who ...

becomes embittered by anguish, adversity, or misfortune, choosing to suffer in silence rather than resolve misunderstandings, or forgive transgressions. He or she is already the source of his or her own misery. Don't make this one the source of yours.

"Like star-crossed lovers, man and God remain separated by suffering – pain becoming the great divide. But it is man, not God, who created the whips, the guns and the gas chambers." -Arianna Huffington

Beware of a
Person Who ...

blames his or her partner for all of the problems in the last relationship. Once we choose to participate in a problem, only 50% of the blame can be pinned on others. To be blameless, one would have to choose not to be a participant at all.

"Attack simply fans the fires of counterattack." -Hugh and Gayle Prather

"You cannot fix what you will not face." -James Baldwin

Beware of a Person Who ...

exercises sole control over your joint financial condition. Never be in the dark about money. Create and execute your own financial plan, otherwise you could end up in foreclosure or out on the street without a warning.

"Strategy is better than strength." -Hausa Proverb

Beware of a
Person Who ...

is co-dependent. This is a self-esteem issue that is best addressed through therapy, self-help books, intervention, or spiritual growth.

Symptoms of co-dependency may include: "low self-esteem, obsession with others, inability to trust, confused emotions, weak personal boundaries, compulsive care-taking, constant denial of the problems caused by co-dependence, and difficulty with sexual issues." -Jody Hayes

Beware of a Person Who ...

nickels and dimes his or her money to death on inexpensive items that don't endure, while complaining about the money you spend on quality items designed to last a lifetime. Class can't be bought for any price, so don't think you can turn a mongrel into a pedigree.

"Under the rule of the "Dollar" human life has fallen to its lowest value." -Charles A. Lindberg, Sr.

Beware of a Person Who ...

does not own, intend to own, or in the very least, is not "actively" saving towards a down payment on a home. A low rent attitude will keep you in a poverty mentality with nothing to pass on to your children.

"Education is the passport to the future, for tomorrow belongs to the people who prepare for it today." -Malcom X

Beware of a Person Who ...

doesn't know a debit from a credit. This person won't be able to balance a checkbook, which could put you in the poor house. Suggest that he or she take a basic bookkeeping, finance or accounting class. If that doesn't work, buy this individual the book "The Millionaire Next Door" and see if he or she heeds its practical advice.

"The Lord will make you so uncomfortable you will end up doing the very thing you fear." -Ruby Dee

Beware of a Person Who ...

confuses love with lust. It will be difficult for such a person to see women or men as little more than sex objects. His or her attitude could affect your image of yourself.

"Love in young men, for the most part is not love but sexual desire, and its accomplishment is the end." - Miguel de Cervantes Saavedra

"Lust, anger & greed, these three are the soul destroying gates of hell." - The Bhagavad-Gita

Beware of a
Person Who ...

does not value higher learning. Lack of education, ignorance, or illiteracy in a society that offers free education for twelve years, while providing grants and low interest loans for higher education, is inexcusable.

"One's work may be finished someday, but one's education, never." -Alexander Dumas

Beware of a
Person Who ...

is addicted to drugs. The substance will always come before you, and nothing short of a spiritual transformation will change this type. Unless you're willing to take backseat to a bad habit, find someone without a drug addiction.

"Addiction robs us of our wholeness. When two people have addictive personalities, they can easily become addicted to each other." -Jody Hayes

Beware of a Person Who ...

wants you to work and put him or her through school. How about both of you working part time, sharing expenses, and going to school together? That way you'll end up equals in education. The reaction to your suggestion will reveal if this person's request was totally selfish.

"Lack of education is an extraordinary handicap when one is being offensive." -Josephine Tey

Beware of a
Person Who ...

can't keep a job and is possibly on a mission to find financial support while he or she "finds himself or herself." If that's the case, this person needs to do that alone. Besides, if you're holding down a nine to five every day, then every "able bodied soul ought to be out looking for a job."

"To be poor and independent is very nearly an impossibility." -William Cobett

Beware of a Person Who ...

seems to know exactly what you should do with your life or career while his or her career is in shambles or at a stand still. Amid the incongruencies between what a person says and does, lies the real truth.

"You must live within your sacred truth." -Hausa Proverb

"There is nothing makes a man suspect much more than to know little." -Francis Bacon

Beware of a Person Who ...

won't let you drive when he or she is in the car with you. Careful that this person doesn't develop a need to be the driving force that controls the rest of your life.

"Before you can drive a car you need a state-approved course of instruction, but driving a car is nothing, nothing compared to living day in and day out with a husband and raising up a new human being." - Anne Tyler

Beware of a
Person Who ...

is a channel surfer who seizes control of the remote, then randomly switches channels while you're in the middle of watching television. Don't expect this type of person to consider your wishes in other areas either.

"A man's home may seem to be his castle on the outside; inside, it is more often his nursery." -Claire Boothe Luce

Beware of a Person Who ...

nags, nags, nags. A person who nags is worst than a leaking roof. Who needs that?

"I have yet to hear a man ask for advice on how to combine marriage and career." -Gloria Steinem

Beware of a Person Who ...

insists that you not wear makeup, dress nicely, or do your hair on weekends. Ask yourself why this person wouldn't want you to look your best every day of the week?

"The most courageous act is still to think for yourself. Aloud."   -Coco Chanel

"Stay away from naggers who complain about the amount of time you take to get beautiful." -Mother Love

Beware of a
Person Who ...

discourages your efforts to lose weight or eat right. Could such a person be insecure and afraid that the opposite sex will look at you? Ask yourself why you would give in, or go along with this subtle form of sabotage?

"A hurtful act is the transference to others of the degradation which we bear on ourselves." -Simone Weil

Beware of a
Person Who ...

expects you to abandon your hobbies or favorite sport to adopt another leisure time activity. While it is good to share and develop common interests, a person should not expect you to give up the things you enjoy because she/he does not enjoy them.

"A desirable woman/man doesn't rearrange his/her priorities every time he/she meets a prospective partner."
-Carter & Sokol

Beware of a Person Who ...

wants you to stop associating with old friends of yours because he or she does not like them. Shouldn't that be your call?

"The abusive person usually has no friends of his/her own and expects his/her partner to supply all his/her emotional needs. Because he/she rarely knows what his/her own needs are, and cannot tell his/her partner what he/she wants, he/she is doomed to fail at an impossible task." -Hawker & Bicehouse

"All love that has not friendship for its base, is like a mansion built upon the sand." -Ella Wheeler Wilcox

Beware of a Person Who ...

awakens you from a much needed rest for trifling reasons. Disregard for another person's sleep is inconsiderate behavior that ends up spilling over into other areas of life.

"Determination to outwit one's situation means that one has no models, only object lessons." -James Baldwin

Beware of a Person Who ...

stays in the room and listens in on your telephone calls or meetings, then tries to dictate how to handle each person or situation. This poor person needs to get some business so that he or she can get out of yours.

"A dictator ... must fool all the people all the time and there's only one way to do that, he must also fool himself." -Somerset Maugham

Beware of a
Person Who ...

not only reads your diary, but confronts you about your journal entries. Ask yourself: did this person's rights get violated too often as a child, or did this individual miss the class on ethics and respecting the privacy or property of others?

"Don't become like the Little Mermaid and lose your voice forever ..." -Carole Lieberman, M.D. & Lisa Cool

Beware of a Person Who ...

goes through the contents of your purse or wallet without permission. (We're talking serious boundary issues here). This is just the beginning of boundary violations.

"It is the business of the very few to be independent; it is a privilege of the strong." - Friedrich Nietzsche

Beware of a Person Who ...

opens your mail as if it had his/her name on the envelope. (Now, we're talking federal offense ...)

"... regard the rights of others as being inherent in them, and not as mere compromise." - Friedrich Nietzsche

Beware of a
Person Who ...

refuses to dress to suit the occasion while accompanying you to an important social or business event.

"Most of the time we are only partially alive. Most of our faculties go on sleeping because they rely on habit which can function without them." -Marcel Proust

Beware of a Person Who ...

forgets your birthday or anniversary and does not bother to make it up to you with a belated present. There's a subtle message somewhere and you need to go about the business of deciphering it.

"Learn to love yourself and you will always be "home" whether there's a man in your life or not." -Carol Lieberman, M.D. & Lisa Cool

Beware of a
Person Who ...

buys shoes or clothing for you in the wrong size. It does not take much effort (only a little forethought) to get your size right.

"How can I set myself free? Who has bound you?" - *Zen*

Beware of a Person Who ...

hates on a whim. Hate is such a devastating, all consuming emotion, no one is really worthy of its expenditure.

"To take hate personally, that is, to take it into my heart and see the attacker with the same eyes in which he sees me is to inflict pain on myself and to extend the world's ancient wound." -Hugh and Gayle Prather

"To become what we are capable of becoming is the only aim of life." -Spinoza

Beware of a Person Who ...

gets up early on the weekend and prepares breakfast for one while you're asleep, then claims that he or she did not know you would be hungry. Who wouldn't be at some point when they wake up? If you accept that lame excuse, you'll eat any old lie this person feeds you.

"Those who are believed to be the most mild and humble are usually the most ambitious and envious." - Spinoza

Beware of a
Person Who ...

wants to become partners in your flourishing business, which does not need a partner. If you let this person in, don't be surprised if he or she tries to take over your company, or offers to buy it out from under you.

"If a man stands high in nature's list, it is natural and inevitable that he should feel solitary ... for if he has to see many other people who are not of like character with himself they will exercise a disturbing influence upon him ... they will rob him of himself and give him nothing to compensate for the loss." - Schopenhauer

Beware of a Person Who ...

at office parties or public gatherings, does not introduce you as a significant other. In general, people are proud to show off, or acknowledge the things they value. Is there a hidden message here?

"Setting limits is meaningless if your [partner] knows you'll forgive any betrayal." -Carole Lieberman, M.D. & Lisa Cool

Beware of a Person Who ...

in the presence of known adversaries or enemies, criticizes or belittles you, then later claims that he or she was only joking. Is the joke on you or the other person; or could this individual be putting you down to put himself or herself up?

"The ego needs recognition. The spirit does not need to thank itself." -Stuart Wilde

Beware of a Person Who ...

thinks that working a 9 to 5 is all that's required in a relationship, even though you also work a nine to five everyday. Even on "Leave It To Beaver" (i.e., the ideal T.V. couple) June Cleaver was a housewife and her husband still helped do dishes after dinner.

"If you pamper him, do it out of love, not desperation. Do it because you sincerely want to, not because you feel he expects it, or will leave if you don't." - Carol Liberman, M.D. and Lisa Cool

Beware of a Person Who ...

disrespects children out of a cultural, patriarchal, or misguided belief that kids should be seen and not heard.

"How sad that man would base an entire civilization ... upon legal ownership and presumed responsibility for children, and then never really get to know their sons and daughters very well." -Phyllis Chesler

"Your children are not your children. They are the sons and daughters of Life's longing for itself...You may give them your love but not your thoughts...For they have their own thoughts...You may strive to be like them, but seek not to make them like you...For life goes not backward nor tarries with yesterday." - Kahlil Gibran

Beware of a Person Who ...

does not genuinely like children or animals, and fails to appreciate the wonder of the world that resides in their innocent eyes. Do not even think about having a family with this person -- the potential damage done to a child from such a union will be irreparable.

"A child is the gateway to the path of empathy and understanding." -Arianna Huffington

"In every child who is born ... the potentiality of the human race is born again; and in him, too, once more, and of each of us, our terrific responsibility toward human life; toward the utmost idea of goodness, of the horror of terror." -James Agee

Beware of a Person Who ...

can eat in front of a hungry child without sharing. If a person is capable of eating while a child stands by begging for a bite, then you haven't a chance in hell of getting this individual to feed your physical or emotional needs.

"If it were natural for fathers to care for their sons, they would not need so many laws commanding them to do so." -Phyllis Chesler

"Children are gifts from God." -Arianna Huffington

Beware of a Person Who ...

is shameless. This type won't know when he or she is behaving badly. No matter how many times you point out the shameless behavior, this person will deny culpability or complain that you're mistaken or wrong.

"A radical is one who speaks the truth." -Charles A. Lindberg, Sr.

Beware of a Person Who ...

has no boundaries, or is unable to distinguish where you begin and he or she ends. This person will feel entitled to impose his or her will on you and expect you to accept it without question or complaint.

"I believe in taking chances ... in gambling with your life ... I've followed my own star." -Lauren Bacal

Beware of a Person Who ...

is a moral moron who, no doubt, is charming, cute and entertaining, yet the rules of society defy his or her best efforts to obey them. Do you really want to share your life with someone who justifies every wrong he or she commits while believing their own pathetic excuses?

"There are some people who will lie to the level of truth, at which point they come to believe their own lies." -Jeanie Morgan Christopher

Beware of a
Person Who ...

religiously avoids open and honest communication. Openness and honesty are the pathways to personal growth and self-actualization. You'll end up arguing about the same issues over and over without ever resolving a thing.

It's definitely not a good sign if a [person] tries to "focus on who is right, or who is going to get their own way, rather than dealing with the disagreement and working out a compromise."   -Hawker & Bicehouse

Beware of a Person Who ...

fails to apologize, even when the situation clearly calls for one. Real men and women will take responsibility for their mistakes by rectifying wrongs against others as soon as they have gained new clarity or insight into the issue.

"A man should never be ashamed to own he has been in the wrong, which is but saying, in other words, that he is wiser today than he was yesterday." - Alexander Pope

Beware of a
Person Who ...

is filled with false pride. Where pride resides, self-improvement dies. Wise King Solomon warned that pride goes before a downfall.

"Egoism -- usually a case of mistaken nonentity." - Barbara Stanwyck

Beware of a Person Who ...

suffers from arrogance mingled with an expanded sense of self worth. Such people won't relate in a positive manner with anyone who challenges their misguided perceptions.

"Self-love is often rather arrogant than blind; it does not hide our faults from ourselves, but persuades us that they escape the notice of others." -Samuel Johnson

"No one has ever yet been hanged for breaking the spirit of the law." -Grover Cleveland

Beware of a Person Who ...

thinks he/she owns his/her spouse or significant other. Undoubtedly, this type confuses people with objects, which means that you will only mean as much as the value placed upon the possession. Love does not seek to own.

"Let your love propel your beloveds into the world and into the full experience of who they are. In this will you have truly loved." -Neale Donald Walsh

"Commitment is the creation of a common end goal for both people involved in a partnership." - Jan Kennedy

Beware of a Person Who ...

needs to be recognized as "winner of the erotic sweepstakes."

"Just as the phallic-snouted wolf can gobble up every female in sight and still be as hungry as ever, your man is gnawed by an insatiable craving for fresh conquests, because he constantly needs more reassurance about his masculinity." -Carole Lieberman, M.D. & Lisa Cool

Beware of a Person Who ...

is physically abusive. Use the one strike rule here.

"The first time a woman is hit she is a victim. The second time she is a volunteer." -Gavin De Becker

Some people draw a comforting distinction between "force" and "violence" ... I refuse to cloud the issue by such word-play. Call an elephant a rabbit only if it gives you comfort to feel that you are about to be trampled to death by a rabbit." -Kenneth Kauda

"Many abusers see themselves as moral people no matter how severe the abuse to their partners." -Hawker & Bicehouse

"Of all animals, man is the only one that is cruel ... It is a trait that is not known in the higher animals." -Mark Twain

Beware of a Person Who ...

wants to control your income or dictate how you spend your earnings, while mismanaging his or her own. Unless such a person is financially secure from wise income investment, you are better off hiring a third party with a proven track record in investment capital to advise you about your money management.

"We are each accountable for our own emotional and financial well being. How can we make someone else happy unless we first nurture our own needs?" - Ruthie O. Grant

Beware of a Person Who ...

is fanatical about religious beliefs; tries to force them on you; knows little or nothing about other religions; or, believes that outsiders are condemned to hell and only those on the inside will be saved. This is a devisive "them" vs. "us" mentality. Historically, many atrocities have been committed in the name of exclusionary religions.Find someone who is spiritual, not religious.

"Cruel persecutions and intolerance are not accidents, but grow out of the very essence of religion, namely, it's absolute claims." -Morris Raphael Cohen

Beware of a Person Who ...

does not know the difference between a religious person and a spiritual being. The former believes in a specific dogma or creed, while the latter embraces all of creation as Holy.

"Religion is mans response to God." -Arianna Huffington

"Man is a religious animal. He is the only religious animal. He is the only animal that has True Religion - several of them. He's the only animal that loves his neighbor as himself and cuts his throat if his theology isn't straight." -Mark Twain

Beware of a Person Who ...

avoids getting in touch with the spiritual side of life. A spiritually bankrupt individual usually gets lost in the pursuit of fragments (such a wealth, fame, sex, etc.) as a substitute for the whole.

"There is something about our modern culture that fears spirituality ... I suspect it is that to admit there is a living God as a force in our lives is to admit that our intellect is not the final source of authority." -Arianna Huffington

Some guys believe that men are "animals trying to be spiritual, when in fact they are spiritual beings fighting against their animalistic selves, or flesh." -Michael Baisden

Beware of a Person Who ...

has mastered the art of seduction. Other than sex, don't expect a deeply rewarding relationship with this type. Sex and games come first on this ones agenda.

"Like a chess grand master, he's explored every imaginable strategy and has dozens of winning moves. He's great at all the little games and intrigues that make romance so much fun and can play a woman's heart with all the skill of a virtuoso." -Carol Liberman, M.D. & Lisa Cool

Beware of a Person Who ...

thinks that therapy is only for crazy people. Each of us have unresolved issues from childhood that could profit from a little professional counseling or self-help therapy. We all belong to the "walking wounded" and would do well to keep in mind that we are "works in progress."

"Life if full of dead people. Empty people who don't know what's wrong with them or, in the most severe cases, that there is even something wrong." -Benilde Little

Beware of a Person Who ...

holds on to an irreconcilable relationship beyond all hope, or good sense, as opposed to dissolving it while there's still a chance to walk away with one's dignity in tact. An individual without dignity will sink to embar-rassing depths.

"After all my erstwhile dear/ my no longer cherished,/ Need we say it was not love,/ Now that love has perished?" -Edna St. Vincent Millay

Beware of a Person Who ...

is too quick to call the relationship quits. This type could be commitment phobic, or have deep-seated abandonment issues that might compel him or her to leave you out of fear of you leaving first.

"A half-hearted commitment to a relationship is no commitment at all. It is a blatant admission that you don't have the other person's welfare at heart." - Jan Kennedy

Beware of a Person Who ...

has no sense of humor. At the right moment a sense of humor is more valuable than gold. He or she will bore you to death.

"He who laughs, lasts." -Mary Pettibone Poole

"Every survival kit should include a sense of humor." -Anonymous

"Laughter is not at all a bad beginning for a friendship, and it is by far the best ending for one." -Oscar Wilde

Beware of a
Person Who ...

does not value the serenity of silence. Maybe this person needs the constant discord of radio, television, or loud people to drown the noise inside his or her head. Unrest will follow this one wherever he or she goes. Are you prepared to give up your peace of mind for some one else's racket?

"Be able to be alone. Lose not the advantage of solitude, and the society of thyself." -Sir Thomas Browne

Beware of a Person Who ...

places his or her primal wants, or animal desires before the real needs of others. The instant this one enters temptation, or becomes dissatisfied with you, monogamy or loyalty will become little more than meaningless words.

"Men have a responsibility to lift themselves above their egotistical and animalistic cravings for sexual and emotional conquests." -Michael Baisden

Beware of a Person Who ...

uses slick, "come on" lines with ease. Don't think you are the first one that this person has tried them on.

"He is every woman's man and every man's woman." - Gaius Scribonius Curio

Beware of a Person Who ...

comes on too strong too soon. This type will burn out quickly once the chase is over, at which point he or she will move on to the next easy conquest.

"Lust is a mysterious wound in the side of humanity; or rather, at the very source of its life! To confound this lust in man with that desire which unites the sexes is like confusing a tumor with the very organ which it devours, a tumor whose deformity horribly reproduces the shape." -Georges Bernanos

Beware of a Person Who ...

while with a crying child, will call for the mother to come running from another room to handle the situation when he could just as easily comfort the child himself. What kind of comfort will he or she be to you in moments of distress?

"It takes a whole village to raise a child." -African Proverb

Beware of a
Person Who ...

will not offer, or refuses to babysit and give the mother of his child a much needed "time-out" to nurture her soul that is being burned out by the never ending needs of a child. Look for the word "selfish" stamped on his soul.

"It's a clear reflection of our values, or lack there of, that in this country we need a license to hunt, drive, or fish, but no license to become a parent and no mandatory classes on parenting." -Ruthie O. Grant

Beware of a Person Who ...

does not believe in planned parenthood. Every child deserves to be born into a family who has prepared for its arrival by planning ahead to meet the child's financial, emotional, and physical needs for love, attention and security.

"In highly evolved societies, "all" births are blessings and "all" mothers and "all" children have their welfare looked after." -Neale Donald Walsch

137

Beware of a Person Who ...

refuses to do his or her equal share of household chores, such as cooking, or cleaning. Those who resented their moms for making them clean up after themselves as a kid, usually do not mature emotionally into responsible adults. They will expect you to fulfill the roles of maid, parent, and lover.

"Never marry a man who hates his mother because he'll end up hating you." -Jill Bennett

Beware of a Person Who ...

when his pregnant wife is having a craving, won't go out at night, or during adverse weather conditions to get her a snack, yet doesn't mind eating what she brings back. He won't be any help once the baby is born. Be prepared to assume the role of single parent with him as a father.

"The present generation, wearied by its chimerical efforts, relapses into complete indolence. Its condition is that of a man who has only fallen asleep towards morning: first of all come great dreams, then a feeling of laziness, and finally a witty or clever excuse for remaining in bed." -Soren Kierkegaard

Beware of a Person Who ...

believes that success is bought at the expense of others. This one won't know the meaning of hard work or sacrifice. And has no clue that any favor gained under fraudulence needs careful guarding to keep.

"All ambitions are lawful except those that climb upward on the miseries or credulities of mankind." - Joseph Conrad

"Do not choose success at the expense of others, but as a tool with which to assist others." -Neale Donald Walsh

Beware of a Person Who ...

has not read any of the great books and has no interest in doing so. People who are able to read and do not read are functional illiterates. Since the actual illiterate is unable to read, at least this type has a legitimate reason for not reading. The functional illiterate has no excuse at all.

"The one thing I regret is that I will never have time to read all of the books I want to read." -Francoise Sagan

Beware of a
Person Who ...

doesn't know Carl Jung from Karl Marx, nor the names of the last few presidents. This one won't be able to distinguish between psychology, socialism and politics. The point is, people without an interest in human nature, psychology, philosophy or sociology will be unable to broaden their understanding of self, the world, and others.

"Just the knowledge that a good book is awaiting at the end of a long day makes that day happier." - Kathleen Norris

Beware of a Person Who ...

is a couch potato. Any potato not worth eating needs to be thrown out.

"Before marriage, a man will go home and lie awake all night thinking about something you said; after marriage, he'll go to sleep before you finish saying it." -Helen Rowland

Beware of a Person Who ...

offers quick, easy excuses for what he or she did or did not do without taking personal responsibility. Any person good at excuses won't be good at anything else.

In a relationship, this type will try desperately to avoid the "I'm not Okay, You're Okay position. The only way he knows to do this is to work as hard as he can blaming her to make her not Okay." -Hawker & Bicehouse

"Accuse. To affirm another's guilt or unworth; most commonly as a justification of ourselves for having wronged him." -Pearl S. Buck

Beware of a
Person Who ...

is impatient. Patience is an important aspect of our relationship with self as well as others, and is a good remedy against discouragement.

"Patience, in many spiritual traditions, is the Devil's favorite way of turning us away from God. Practicing patience is nothing less than practicing cooperation with God's will." -Arianna Huffington

"You get a chicken from an egg by hatching it, not smashing it." -Proverb

Beware of a Person Who ...

believes there is no such thing as date rape. This type of person will confuse familiarity with territorial rights. He or she may also feel that any woman who dresses provocatively, or, who is out alone at night is asking to be raped.

"A man assumes that a woman's refusal is just part of a game. Or, at any rate, a lot of men assume that. When a man says no, it's no. When a woman says no, it's yes, or at least maybe. There is even a joke to that effect. And little by little, women begin to believe in this view of themselves." -Erica Jong

Beware of a Person Who ...

affectionately refers to you as his or her "pet." Be careful that this type does not start treating you like one as well.

"...He may indeed be an individual whose affection is dependent upon her being a pet, who lacks the capacity to respect her strength, independence and individuality ... It is their attachment to us rather than their independence from us that we value in our pets." - M. Scott Peck

"The only cure for contempt is counter-contempt." - H. L. Mencken

Beware of a
Person Who ...

was abused or molested as a child and never sought help (either on his or her own or professionally). Chances are this one will repeat the pattern since the "sins of the fathers are often visited upon the sons."

"Sexual abuse of children now presents society with the ultimate crisis of patriarchy, when children refuse to protect their fathers by keeping secrets." - Beatrix Campbell

Beware of a
Person Who ...

is delusional and irrationally believes that everybody else is wrong while he or she alone is absolutely right. Watch out for people who believe in absolutes.

"Steer clear of those with irrational behavior. If you hang around with crazymakers for too long, you'll end up modeling their behavior, accepting it as normal, or joining them in their delusions!" - Ruthie O. Grant

Beware of a Person Who ...

believes in strict gender roles for men and women. This type will define what's ladylike or masculine, and what's not, then restrict you from activities he or she deems unsuitable for men or women. Reinvent yourself. Be your own man or woman.

"Men [and women] who are abusive usually have rigidly defined sex roles. They have iron clad rules for what women should do and what men should do." - Hawker & Bicehouse

Beware of a Person Who ...

thinks that education ends with graduation from high school or college. Learning is a life long pursuit. Failure or refusal to exercise the freedom to grow puts us in a prison of our own making.

"When the freedom they wished for most was freedom from responsibility, then Athens ceased to be free and was never free again." - Edith Hamilton

Beware of a Person Who ...

thinks that personal growth is measured in inches.

"The fatal metaphor of progress, which means leaving things behind us, has utterly obscured the real idea of growth, which means leaving things inside us." -G. K. Chesterton

Beware of a Person Who ...

disagrees for the sake of being disagreeable. If contention or confusion is your game, this is your man or woman.

"If at all possible be on good terms with all people."
-Anonymous

Beware of a Person Who ...

can only see one option, one opinion or one world viewpoint: his or her own. In this person's mind, he or she is the only one worthy of gain. Don't expect any win/win situations with this one.

"In the vain laughter of folly wisdom hears half its applause." -George Eliot

Beware of a
Person Who ...

gets out of the car empty handed, leaving you to struggle with an arm load of bags or luggage.

"All which I abandon, all which I give, I enjoy in a higher manner through the fact that I give it away ... to give is to enjoy possessively the object which one gives." -Jean-Paul Satre

Beware of a
Person Who ...

*will awaken a small child from sleep
and make the toddler walk to bed
crying when this individual could just
as easily have carried the child to
bed. Inconsideration is the operative
word here.*

*"I am not sure how many "sins" I would recognize in
the world. Some would surely be defused by changed
circumstances. But I can imagine none that is more
irredeemably sinful than the betrayal, or the
exploitation, of the young by those who should care
for them." -Elizabeth Janeway*

Beware of a Person Who ...

after a date, drives off without walking you to your door, or seeing you safely inside. It's "out of sight, out of mind for this one."

"The study of history is useful to the historian by teaching him his ignorance of women." -Henry Adams

"Our doubts are traitors, and make us lose the good we often might win by fearing to attempt." - Shakespeare

Beware of a Person Who ...

fails to offer his jacket when he sees you shivering and your teeth chattering. Contrary to popular opinion, chivalry is not dead.

"When a man opens the car door for his wife, it's either a new car or a new wife." -Prince Philip, Duke of Edinburgh

Beware of a
Person Who ...

*borrows money from you. Period!
Regardless of the reason, borrowing
money can destroy even the best of
relationships, unless the money is paid
back.*

"Neither a borrower nor a lender be." -Ben Franklin

Beware of a
Person Who ...

gives you money, or a gift, then turns around and borrows it back at a later date.

"Beware of communal gift givers -- they can only see in terms of "mine" and "ours. Nothing they give you will truly be yours." -Ruthie O. Grant

"With that gift he decided he didn't owe anybody anything ... So he extended his debtlessness to other people by helping them pay off whatever they owed in misery ... gave them their own bill of sale, so to speak: 'You paid it; now life owes you.' - Toni Morrison (from "Beloved")

Beware of a Person Who ...

begrudges the time you spend alone or with others. Everyone needs their own space. If he or she does not honor this fundamental principle, such an individual won't understand the concept either.

"All things must be set right in yourself first before you can rightly assist others towards attaining the same state." -Law

Beware of a Person Who ...

gives you his or her work number, voice mail number, or pager number and tells you that he or she can't be reached at home. (Gee, I wonder why? Could it be that this person is living with someone? What does your intuition tell you?)

"Intuition is the clear conception of the whole at once." -Lavater

Beware of a
Person Who ...

promises that he or she is going to divorce his wife or husband as soon as the children are older; or, tells you that he's only with his wife because it's cheaper to keep her, or because she cannot afford to leave him.

"The majority of men who have affairs end up staying with their current spouse ...As long as he has his wife, your lover always has a safety net to land in should your love affair collapse ... It's gratifying to him to have two women competing over him -- even if one of them doesn't realize it." -Carole Lieberman, M.D. & Lisa Cool

Beware of a
Person Who ...

needs you as a pretty ornament on his arm to make him look good in public. The flip side of that is true too: don't choose a pretty man who's only good for one thing.

"If I lead another life ... I shall take precious good care not to hang myself around any man's neck either as a locket or a millstone." -Jane Carlyle

Beware of a Person Who ...

is anxious to have an affair with you, but lets you know up front that he has no intention of divorcing his wife or her husband. Now, why would you settle for being the "other" woman or man when you could be Queen or "King of the Heap?"

"Every man wants a woman to appeal to his better side, his noble instincts and his higher nature --and another woman to help him forget them." -Helen Rowland

Beware of a
Person Who ...

bad mouths his wife or her husband to you and then complains that he or she is not getting enough sex at home. This person wouldn't be looking for a little sympathy sex, eh?

"Men or women who are unhappy, like men or women who sleep badly, are always proud of the fact." - Bertrand Russell

"A woman one loves rarely suffices for all our needs, so we deceive her with another whom we do not love." - Marcel Proust

Beware of a
Person Who ...

is a chronic or habitual liar. A liar can't be believed even when he or she tells the truth. Do you really want to be with someone you can't believe or trust? Since the eyes are the window to the soul, see if this one can look you in the eye while lying.

"Men's lies tend to be protective of their own freedom and autonomy ... When we confront the liar, he acts like we're crazy and says something that makes us wonder how we ever could have thought him a liar." -Dory Hollander, Ph.D.

Beware of a
Person Who ...

is intolerant of other people's religions, cultures, traditions or sexual preferences. Rest assured that this one will be intolerant of the subtle differences between the two of you as well.

"Prejudices, it is well known, are most difficult to eradicate from the heart whose soil has never been loosened or fertilized by [a liberal] education; they grow firm there, firm as weeds among stones." - Charlotte Bronte

Beware of a
Person Who ...

refuses to acknowledge or accept new ideas and concepts that differ greatly from those he or she has held since childhood. Chances are this type is also immature, rigid, and inflexible, which means that he or she won't bend; this one would rather see you break first.

"You can't shake hands with a clenched fist." -Indira Gandhi

Beware of a
Person Who ...

is highly critical of others. Eventually, even if it's behind your back, this type of person will criticize you with the same easy abandonment.

"Why are women so much more interesting to men than men are to women?" - Virginia Woolf

Beware of a
Person Who ...

wears cheap shoes. Chances are, he or she won't have good taste in other areas either.

"I'd rather see a fifteen year old pair of quality shoes on a man than cheap shoes. Same goes for clothes. If I was your Mama, I wouldn't want you bringin' no raggedy-ass, soleless man home to me! Period. " - Mother Love

Beware of a
Person Who ...

is a "quick fix reader" who only scans newspapers, magazines or work related materials. This form of reading does not render one literate.

"If you're a reader, and he or she is not, rest assured that this person will run interference on your reading time so that you'll have more time to do important things with him/or her like hold their beer while they watch television." -Ruthie O. Grant

Beware of a Person Who ...

is in awe of, or intimidated by your level of education and intelligence. Has this person ever thought of developing or expanding his or her own horizons? This type will be emotionally needy and insecure. Typically, the most balanced relationships are between equals.

"The bitterest creature under heaven is the wife who discovers that her husband's bravery is only bravado, that his strength is only a uniform, that his power is but a gun in the hands of a fool." -Pearl S. Buck

Beware of a
Person Who ...

feels threatened by your income level. Since limits are self-imposed, a man or woman will only earn as much money as he or she feels deserving of. A limited attitude will hold you back by association since it breeds assimilation.

"I think there is something degrading about having a husband for a rival. It's humiliating if you fail and common place if you succeed." -Christopher Hampton

Beware of a Person Who ...

brags or boasts about earnings, or how important his or her job is.

"Glamorizing work is probably the most impression-management ploy. If what he does for a living defines him, upping his job status increases his market value. The hyped-up resume has become to the courting ritual what fake I.D.'s used to be for the under age drinking crowd - an entry card." -Dory Hollander, Ph.D

Beware of a Person Who ...

is overly impressed with his or her parents' wealth or accomplishments. Chances are this individual will never meet or exceed the success level of the parents.

"God bless the child that's got his own." -Billie Holliday

Beware of a Person Who ...

expects to succeed off of your success. Those who have limited faith in their ability to succeed in life will pull you down with their negative belief patterns.

"Do not become unevenly yoked." - New Testament.

"We all need money, but there are degrees of desperation." - Anthony Burgess

"Money is better than poverty, if only for financial reasons." - Unknown

Beware of a Person Who ...

is embarrassed by, or uncomfortable with a casual kiss, a hug, or holding hands in public. Is this person afraid that someone he or she knows will see the two of you together? Or does this one believe that public displays of affection will lead onlookers to believe that he or she is not available?

"The tragedy of machismo is that a man is never quite man enough. -Germaine Greer

Beware of a
Person Who ...

is quick to give men credit for the greatest and highest accomplishments in society, while relegating women to secondary positions of status.   This is patriarchal mind conditioning at its worst.

"Ginger Rogers did everything Fred Astaire did, but she did it backwards and in high heels."   -Faith Whittlesey

"The man who never alters his opinion is like standing water and breeds reptiles of the mind." -William Blake

Beware of a
Person Who ...

spends a disproportionate amount of his or her income on clothing, cars, or non-income producing hobbies. Watch out: this one's bills and necessities might take a back seat to his or her spending.

"No other man-made device since the shields and lances of the ancient knights fulfills a man's ego like an automobile." -Sir William Rootes

Beware of a Person Who ...

gambles. He or she may be generous upon winning, but when this type loses, he or she will expect you to return the cash. So, beware of those bearing gifts gained from gambling.

"Show me a gambler and I'll show you a loser, show me a hero and I'll show you a corpse." -Mario Puzo

"Someone once asked me why women don't gamble as much as men do, and I gave the common-sensical reply that we don't have as much money. That was a true but incomplete answer. In fact, women's total instinct for gambling is satisfied by marriage." - Gloria Steinem

Beware of a
Person Who ...

is apathetic and without inner motivation. This type will not believe that one person can actually make a difference, in spite of what individual people, like Harriet Tubman, Einstein, Ghandi, Jesus, Buddha, and Martin Luther King, Jr. did to uplift society.

"Government can make good laws, but cannot make men and women good. Without good men and women we cannot have a good society. We become good by practicing and doing good." -Arianna Huffington

Beware of a
Person Who ...

thinks it's his or her job to point out to others the error of their ways, whether they want to hear it or not. Since everyone has to learn from their own mistakes, advice is best offered when asked.

"The passion for setting people right is in itself an afflictive disease." -Marianne Moore

Beware of a
Person Who ...

is obsessed with pornographic materials, movies, songs, or books that degrade or exploit women, children, or men.

"It is psychologically difficult for a person to restrict his or her [depravity, or] violence to socially acceptable outlets and not to generalize it to others."
-Alyce LaViolette

Beware of a
Person Who ...

cries easily. Be sure that the tears are not self-serving. This could be a manipulative ploy. If an individual is genuinely sensitive, he or she will cry during movies, or out of empathy with others who are emotionally distraught.

"It's true that men who cry are sensitive to and in touch with their feelings, but the only feelings they tend to be sensitive to and in touch with are their own." -Nora Ephron

Beware of a Person Who ...

spends more time in front of the mirror than you do.

"Glamorous, good-looking men are like delicate house plants -- they need constant attention, and for that maybe you'll get flowers once a year." -Carter & Sokol

"If he spends more time getting ready to go out than you do, he probably thinks he's prettier than you. I always say: Give me a man who can get dressed and pressed in 20 minutes." -Mother Love

Beware of a Person Who ...

does not pay adequate child support, participate actively in the lives of his children; or, is divorced and living well while his children and ex-wife live poorly. If he doesn't take loving care of his offspring, he won't care much for you either.

"The true index of a man's character is the health of his wife." -Cyril Connolly

Beware of a Person Who ...

who has stalked his or her "ex" or anyone else. Warning signs include: overly possessiveness; jealousy of your male friends; attempts to isolate you from others; poor social skills; inability to form peer friendships; or, grew up in a family that was physically or emotionally abusive. ("Essence" Oct. '93)

Stalkers "are often vindictive ... and quick to anger ... and are preoccupied with violent ideas and fantasies, always like to dominate and are cruel without remorse." -Lenore Walker

Beware of a Person Who ...

stares lasciviously at every attractive person of the opposite sex who passes by as if you were not even present. Have more respect for yourself than to sit there while this person ogles the opposite sex. Leave the minute his or her stare becomes glued on another person to the exclusion of you. Don't you deserve someone who can't take his or her eyes off of you?

"Trust thyself; every heart vibrates to that iron string." -Ralph Waldo Emerson

Beware of a Person Who ...

refers to women as "Bitches," "Whores," or "Sluts" based on the way they are dressed or their looks. Labels are earned according to deed, not dress or outward appearance.

"The argument between wives and whores is an old one; each one thinking that whatever she is, at least she is not the other." -Andrea Dworkin

"Forget not that modesty is for a shield against the eye of the unclean." -Kahlil Gibran

Beware of a Person Who ...

clings to bad behavior, out-dated thinking, and old things. Such individuals cannot call themselves adults until they relinquish childish concepts and embrace the pain of loss, separation and detachment.

"Death of the old is birth of the new ... All pathologic depressions involve some blockage in the giving up process .. failing to negotiate any crisis, to truly grow up, and to experience the joyful sense of rebirth that accompanies the successful transition into greater maturity." -M. Scott Peck

Beware of a
Person Who ...

is more concerned about how he or she "appears" to be in front of others in to gain acceptance by them. What matters is making a genuine effort to become the real man or woman that one pretends to be in public.

"Hypocrisy is the most difficult and nerve-racking vice that any man can pursue; it needs an unceasing vigilance and a rare detachment of spirit. It cannot, like adultery or gluttony, be practiced at spare moments; it is a whole-time job." -W. Somerset Maugham

"How dwarfed against his manliness she sees the poor pretension, the wants, the aims, the follies, born of fashion and convention." -John Greenleaf Whittier

Beware of a Person Who ...

pays no attention to details. This one will be in perpetual "rough draft" when you need him or her to be polished and ready for presentation.

"No barber shaves so close but another finds his work." -English Proverb

"One might call habit a moral friction; something that prevents the mind from gliding over things but connects it with them and makes it hard for it to free itself from them." - G.C. Lichtenberg

Beware of a
Person Who ...

does not follow his or her bliss. This type will experience feelings of "quiet desperation" and misery without understanding why.

"Condition, circumstance, is not the thing; bliss is the same in subject or in king." - Alexander Pope

Beware of a Person Who ...

can only recite poetry from pop songs; or, believes that real men or women don't read or write poetry.

"Poetry is the voice of pain and beauty crying out simultaneously, creating a momentary melody captured in ink on the pages of eternity." -Ruthie O. Grant

Beware of a Person Who ...

demands your total and complete dependence upon him or her even though you are quite capable or willing to do for yourself. Strive to give yourself the gift of financial, emotional and intellectual independence and self sufficiency.

"To depend upon a profession is a less odious form of slavery than to depend upon a father [or husband]." - Virginia Woolf

"The more independent you want to be, the more generous you must be with yourself." -Diane von Furstenberg

Beware of a Person Who ...

does not understand or honor the significance of the poet's words: "I am the Master of my fate. I am the Captain of my soul."

"It is necessary to the happiness of a man that he be mentally faithful to himself." -Thomas Paine

"So you protected yourself and loved small. Picked the tiniest stars out of the sky to own ... to get to the place where you could love anything you chose -- not to need permission for desire -- well now that was freedom." -Toni Morrison (from "Beloved")

Beware of a Person Who ...

never comes up with new, or innovative interludes to keep the flame burning brightly in your relationship; and doesn't even have the good taste to buy a faux fireplace to add a bit of ambiance to his or her abode.

"Husbands are like fires.   They go out when unattended." -Zsa Zsa Gabor

"If passion dies or is denied, we are partly dead and soon, come what may, we will be wholly so." -John Boorman

Beware of a Person Who ...

takes credit for your ideas or work. Need I say more?

"Unless both parties have a commitment to support their MUTUAL growth and well-being, it is unlikely that either party will ever feel really good about the relationship." ("The Venus Factor") -Jan Kennedy

Beware of a
Person Who ...

is jealous. No! It's not cute. And no, it does not mean that he or she is desperately in love with you! It simply means that this individual is desperate.

"Jealousy indicates the level of insecurity a man feels and the degree of control he feels entitled to." - Hawker & Bicehouse

"Jealousy is all the fun you think they had." -Erica Jong

"Jealousy, that dragon which slays love under the pretense of keeping it alive." -Havelock Ellis

Beware of a Person Who ...

does not have an intelligent or clearly defined idea of what he or she wants or needs most from a relationship. This person will expect you to magically intuit his or her needs without ever clearly communicating them to you.

"On the first date, share your heirachy of values and expectations with your date. Then compare lists to find out what you have in common. Physical attraction is not enough to sustain a long term relationship -- you need common interests to build upon." -Ruthie O. Grant

Beware of a
Person Who ...

views anger as a negative or destructive emotion and rejects it in himself and others. This person won't be able to deal constructively with situations that require the energy of anger to shape a solution.

"Anger never hurt anyone. It's the choices" made when angry that hurt. -Hawker & Bicehouse

PART II
Understanding Toxic Personalities

Good people are rarely suspicious: they cannot imagine others doing the things they themselves are incapable of doing ... The normal are inclined to visualize the [psychopath] as one who's as monstrous in appearance as he is in mind, which is about as far from the truth as one could well get ... These monsters of real life presented a more convincing picture of viture than virtue presented of itself.

    -William March, "The Bad Seed"

Although no one is immune to the devious machinations of the psychopath, there are some things you can do to reduce your vulnerability.

    -Robert D. Hare, Phd, "Without Conscience"

THE SOCIAL RELEVANCE OF UNDERSTANDING TOXIC PERSONALITIES
aka Personality Disorders, Sociopaths, or Psychopaths

Very few psychopaths commit crimes [of torture and mutilation]. Their callousness typically emerges in less dramatic, though still devastating ways: parasitically bleeding other people of their possessions, savings, and dignity; aggressively doing and taking what they want; shamefully neglecting the physical and emotional welfare of their families; engaging in an unending series of casual, impersonal, and trivial sexual relationships; and so forth (Hare 45).
-Dr. Robert D. Hare <u>Without Conscience</u>

The total pattern of the psychopath's personality differentiates him from the normal criminal. His aggression is more intense, his impulsivity more pronounced, his emotional reactions more shallow. His guiltlessness, however, is the critical distinguishing trait. The normal criminal has an internalized, albeit warped, set of values. If he violates these standards he feels guilt.
-McCord and McCord. The Psychopath: An Essay on the Criminal Mind

Dr. Gregory W. Lester, an expert on personality disorders, feels that it is important to understand personality disorders because they make up 16-20% of the general population and appear to be rapidly increasing in prevalence. They also make up 59-100% of the clinical population; are associated with spouse abuse 80-90% of the time; are connected to compulsive addictive disorders nearly 65% of the time; and, some categories have suicide and homicide rates far above that of the general population. They are also nearly always underestimated and underidentified by social workers and other health and mental health professionals (Lester1-2). ***Gregory W. Lester, PhD*** gives workshops and seminars all over the U.S. to social workers and mental health professionals who treat personality disorders and is the author of Personality Disorders in Social Work Practice.

The Diagnostic Statistical Manual (DSM-IV) in 1994, defined a personality disorder as "***an enduring pattern of inner experience and behavior that deviates markedly from the expectations of the individual's culture, is pervasive and inflexible, has an onset in adolescence or early adulthood, is stable over time, and leads to distress or impairment***."

The three personality disorders that cause the most chaos in relationships are: ***Narcissistic*** (NPD), ***Borderline*** (BPD), and ***Antisocial*** (APD). All three have overlapping traits. Since there are eleven different personality disorders listed in the DSM-IV, the author grouped the three most troublesome ones under the term "toxic personalities" for ease of reference in this book.

Definition of Narcissistic: The narcissistic perso-nality disorder can be recognized by a "grandiose sense of self-importance; recurrent fantasies of unlimited success, power, brilliance, beauty or ideal love; a craving for constant attention and admiration; feelings of rage, humiliation, or haughty indifference when criticized or defeated; and at least two of the following: a sense of en-titlement; exploitiveness, the tendency to take advantage of others and to disregard their rights; oscillation between extreme over idealization and devaluation of others; and lack of empathy, meaning not just an inability to recognize how others feel, but often an inability to see that others have feelings at all" (Pines C-1).

Sanford and Donovan, in their book <u>Women and Self-Esteem</u>, point out that the difficulty with identifying narcissistic personality disorders in males as a serious societal problem that needs addressing, is due to our double standard prevalent in a patriarchal society wherein the narcissistic traits of males with personality disorders are applauded and often viewed as distinctively masculine traits or signs of self worth in men. "Traditionally, among white men these [narcissistic] traits have been considered beyond criticism, even admirable [and] ... while not all men display [narcissistic] traits, it nonetheless remains true that white men in Western culture have been displaying these traits for centuries" (Sanford & Donovan 10-11).

The DSM-IV Definition of *Borderline Personality Disorder* is: A pervasive pattern of instability of interpersonal relationships, self-image, and affects, and marked impulsivity beginning by early adulthood and present in a variety of contexts, as indicated by five (or more) of the following: (1) frantic efforts to avoid real or imagined abandonment; (2) a pattern of unstable and intense interpersonal relationships character-ized by alternating between extremes of idealization and devaluation; (3) identity distur-bance: markedly and persistently unstable self-image or sense of self; (4) impulsivity in at least two areas that are potentially self-damaging (e.g., spending, sex, substance abuse, reckless driving, binge eating); (5) recurrent suicidal behavior, gestures, or threats, or self mutilating behavior; (6) affective instability due to a marked reactivity of mood (e.g., intense episodic dysphoria, irritability, or anxiety usually lasting a few hours and only rarely more than a few days); (7) chronic feelings of emptiness; (8) inappropriate, intense anger or difficulty controlling anger (e.g., frequent displays of temper, constant anger, recurrent physical fights); (9) transient, stress-related paranoid ideation or severe dissociative symptoms."

The DSM-IV Definition of *Antisocial Personality Disorder* is:

(A) A pervasive pattern of disregard for and a violation of the rights of others occurring since age 15 years as indicated by three (or more) of the following:

(1) failure to conform to social norms with respect to lawful behaviors as indicated by repeatedly performing acts that are grounds for arrest; (2) deceitfulness, as indicated by repeated lying, use of aliases or conning others for personal

profit or pleasure; (3) impulsivity or failure to plan ahead; (4) irritability and aggressiveness, as indicated by repeated physical fights or assaults; (5) reckless disregard for safety of self or others; (6) consistent irresponsibility, as indicated by repeated failure to sustain consistent work behavior or honor financial obligations; (7) lack of remorse, as indicated by being indifferent to or rationalizing having hurt, mistreated or stolen from another.

(B) The individual is at least age 18 years.

(C) There is evidence of Conduct Disorder with onset before age 15 years.

(D) The occurrence of antisocial behavior is not exclusively during the course of Schizophrenia or a Manic Episode.

HISTORY OF PERSONALITY DISORDERS

Antisocial personality disorders are also referred to as psychopaths, sociopaths, or dissocial personalities. Descriptions of antisocial personality can be traced to early Greek literature. It was the prototypical personality disorder, in that the term "psychopath" originally referred to personality disorders in general (Sperry 15). In the early 1900's there were only two categories of psychiatric illnesses: psychotic, which involved distortions of perception; and, neurotic which involved an internal conflict that produces distress but no distortion of reality. Over time, some patients were observed who did not fit these categories. Some appeared psychotic but were less out of contact with reality and appeared to function at some level but did not deteriorate. Nearly all were treatment failures and produced confusion and upset in others, including professionals. It was not until the 1960's that these patients began to be seen as different and became the category now known as personality disorders which did not fully crystallize until the late 1970's. Pre-1980 diagnostic and psychiatric literature contained no distinct category for these individuals. They were seen as severe neurotic or mild psychotic disorders.

The DSM-I, the first formal diagnostic manual of the American Psychiatric Association, offered no distinct diagnosis for these individuals.

The DSM-II, released in 1968, offered no specific diagnostic criteria and gave no diagnostic formulations based on clinical trials. The DSM-III, released in 1980, acknowledged personality disorders to be different from psychiatric disturbances. It was acknowledged that they could coexist with psychiatric disturbances as well as occur without other psychiatric disturbances.

In 1941, the psychopathic personality was described as having "superficial charm, unreliability, poor judgment, and a lack of social responsibility, guilt, anxiety or remorse." The term was replaced by sociopath to reflect the social rather than purely psychological origins of the disorder (more on that later). The DSM-III added "lacks remorse" although it did not focus on the incapacity for love, or failure to learn from experience. The DSM-IV emphasizes the psychopathic traits while deemphasizing the criminal behavior of antisocial personality disorders. (Sperry 15).

Sociopath vs. Psychopath: Sometimes **sociopath** is used instead of **psychopath** because the psychopath is often *confused with psychotic* and sociopath is "less likely to be confused with psychoticism or insanity." Clinicians who "believe that the syndrome is forged entirely by **social forces** and early experiences prefer the term **sociopath;** whereas those ... who feel that **psychological, biological** and **genetic** factors also contribute to the development of the syndrome generally use the term **psychopath** (Hare 23-24). "

Dr. Robert D. Hare, author of Without Conscience is an expert on psychopaths. He developed the **Psychopathy Checklist**, which is a highly reliable and predictive tool used by clinicians. Hare cautions one not to use the following symptoms to diagnose yourself or others because people who are not psychopaths may have some of the symptoms [more on that later] (Hare 34):

PSYCHOPATHY CHECKLIST

Emotional/Interpersonal	Social Deviance
-Glib and superficial	-Impulsive
-Egocentric and grandiose	-Poor behavior controls
-Lack of remorse or guilt	-Need for excitement
-Lack of empathy	-Lack of responsibility
-Deceitful and manipulative	-Early behavior problems
-Shallow emotions	-Adult antisocial behavior

PERSONALITY STYLE vs. PERSONALITY DISORDER

Note that there is a difference between a perso-nality *"style"* and a personality *"disorder."* For example, someone with a style similar to an *antisocial personality disorder (APD)* tends to be "silver-tongued, gifted in the art of winning friends;" whereas, the actual *APD* "has no regard for the truth, as indicated by repeated lying, use of aliases, or "conning" others for personal profit or pleasure." Someone with the *style* would prefer "free-lancer living, and live-well behavior;" whereas, the *APD* is "unable to sustain consistent work by their talents, skills, ingenuity or wits" (Sperry 17).

Someone with a *style* similar to a *borderline personality disorder (BPD)* would "tend to experience passionate focused attachments in all relationships. Nothing in the relationship is taken lightly;" whereas, the *BPD* exhibits a "pattern of unstable and intense relationships noted by alternating between extremes of lover idealization and devaluation" (Sperry 54).

Someone with the style of the *narcissistic personality disorder (NPD)* "although emotionally vulnerable to negative assessments and feelings of others, can hurdle these with style and grace." However, the *NPD* tends to "react to criticism with feelings of rage, stress, or humiliation (even if not expressed)" (Sperry 115).

This comparison/contrast is helpful in pointing out that an individual can exhibit the *style* of a personality disorder without actually *being* a personality disorder, which is why it is important to note the difference between a personality "style" and a personality "disorder" and not confuse the two. The following comparison will enable one to further distinguish between the two.

THE SOCIAL PERSONALITY VS. THE ANTISOCIAL PERSONALITY

L. Ron Hubbard, in his booklet <u>The Cause of Suppression</u> says that "the social personality operates on the basis of the greatest good ... whereas, the antisocial personality really and covertly wants others to succumb. The social personality wants to survive and wants others to survive, whereas the antisocial personality is very clever in making others do very badly indeed ... All majority rules, civilizing intentions, and even the human race will fail unless one can identify and thwart the antisocial personalities and help and forward the social personalities in the society ... Government is only dangerous when it can be employed by and for antisocial personalities ... Unless we can detect the social personality and hold him (or her) safe from undue restraint, and detect also the antisocial and restrain him or her, our society will go on suffering from insanity, criminality and war, and civilization will not endure."

All one has to do is look at criminals, corrupt government officials, the heads of many national corporations and countries, and dictators around the world to see the term "antisocial" in full operation. Toxic personalities operate against the good of the planet and humanity, have no conscience, are uncaring about the consequences of their actions toward others, and will pretend that their aims and goals have the best interests of others at heart when, in reality, these individuals are covertly driven by self serving interests.

HUBBARD'S TRAITS OF THE SOCIAL PERSONALITY

- Is eager to relay good news and reluctant to relay bad.
- Is specific in relating circumstances or sources of information.
- Passes along communication without much alteration, and if deleting anything, tends to delete hurtful or injurious matters. Responds well to treatment and social reform. Friends and associates tend to be well, happy and of good morale
- Tends to select correct targets for correction.
- Tends to complete what he or she starts.
- Is ashamed of misdeeds and does not brag about them. Takes responsibility for correcting mistakes and for learning from experience.
- Supports constructive groups and tends to protest or resist destructive groups.

- Helps others and actively resists acts which harm others.
- Respects the person and property of others. Frowns upon theft or misuse of the property of others.

Hubbard's research reveals that "The basic reason the antisocial personality behaves as he or she does lies in a **hidden terror of others.** Every other being is an enemy to be covertly or overtly destroyed. The fixation is that survival itself depends on keeping others down or keeping people ignorant. If anyone were to promise to make others stronger or brighter, the antisocial personality suffers the utmost agony of personal danger. The antisocial person reasons that if they are in this much trouble with people around them weak or stupid, they would perish should anyone around them become strong or bright. They feel threatened by anyone who is smarter or more competent. Such a person has no trust to the point of terror. This is usually masked and unrevealed. **The bulk of such people exhibit no outward sign of insanity. They appear quite rational. They can be very convincing**."

According to Donald G. Dutton's research in "The Domestic Assault of Women," 85% of males in anger management or domestic violence treatment programs have personality disorders (many have a combination of personality disorders.)

WARNING SIGNS TO WATCH FOR

Because toxic personalities are masters at manipulation and deception, initially, it is difficult to realize that one is dealing with one. There are, however, red flags or warning signs that one can watch for. In particular: duplicity; inconsistencies between what a person says and does; making excuses or changing the subject when caught in a lie; showing no shame or emotion when caught in a compromising or embarrassing situation; failing to answer the question posed, or answering in such a way that is nonresponsive to the question; an "uncanny ability" to "detect our vulnerabilities and to push the right buttons"; a tendency to see "any social exchange as a feeding opportunity, a contest, or a test of wills, in which there can be only one winner"; those motivated to "manipulate and take ruthlessly and without remorse"; individuals who "understand the intellectual rules of the game but the emotional rules are lost on them"; those with speech that is poorly connected, tangential, filled with contradictions, evasiveness, rationalizations, or excuses; individuals who use more empty hand gestures than normal during speech or pauses in speech. This tendency "appears to reflect difficulty in converting thoughts and feelings into speech ... emotion is like a second language to the psychopath   (Hare 141-147, 135)."

Any combination of the above can be warning signs that you might be dealing with a personality disorder.   Proceed with caution, or avoid all together.

PROBLEMS WITH DIAGNOSIS

"Defining the symptoms of personality disorders is more challenging than defining symptoms for the clinical disorders" because "personality traits, such as vanity, inappropriate anger, dependency, and so on, are harder to define." For example, with clinical disorders, it is easy to receive answers to questions like "Do you cry a lot?" or "Do you get the shakes?" However, it is difficult for an interviewer who is trying to diagnose a personality disorder to ask "Are you vain or demanding" or "Are you manipulative and exploitative?" (Benjamin 5).

Dr. Lorna Smith Benjamin created a *Structural Analysis of Social Behavior (SASB)* since some of the disorders have the same overlapping traits. For example, the DSM lists anger as an issue with BPD, APD and NPD. Thus, Dr. Benjamin specifies a "particular interpersonal context for each of the symptoms defining the respective personality disorders." For example, the *borderline* personality disorder's anger is recklessly executed and is usually inspired by "panic over loss or abandonment" and wondering whether the caregiver or lover "cares and gives" enough. The *antisocial* personality disorder's anger is "cold and functional" and is executed without remorse or care for damage inflicted and is designed to maintain or demonstrate control; whereas. *Narcissistic* personality disorders feel "entitled" and will become angry if their needs are not automatically filled—if the world does not "fall at their feet." The SASB approach diminishes the overlap problem greatly by putting anger into different contexts which have different intended outcomes for the different disorders (Benjamin 8-9).

Moreover, Benjamin points out that after reading the DSM, one can walk away believing that "he or she has nearly every personality disorder there is. Probably any remaining disorders can be assigned to one's spouse. The symptoms of personality disorders can be universally human." Benjamin stresses, however, that "personality disorders have a serious social impact" because "nearly *one in every 10 adults* in the general population, and over *one-half those in treated populations*, may be expected to suffer from one of the personality disorders." (Benjamin 3-4).

Dr. Lester finds that personality disorders "generally create the most difficult and troublesome health care cases and are responsible for many, if not most, treatment and case management failures" (Lester 1). His findings also show that personality disorders are "nearly always underestimated and under-identified by social workers and other health and mental health professionals and are extremely difficult to successfully manage and treat because they are largely unaffected by traditional treatment and behavioral management approaches" (Lester 2).

This is a pressing societal problem because personality disorders represent a "risk factor for other serious life and medical problems" in that they are responsible for marital dysfunction, child abuse, and medical non-compliance." Lester lists the following ways in which personality disorders are unique, which reveals the difficulty in identifying and dealing with them. Individuals with personality disorders:

- Lack ability to productively use insight;
- Do not respond to traditional therapeutic techniques;
- Often present vague, general, indistinct, chronic complaints of distress;
- Fail to comply with treatment or management regimes;
- Cannot see the role their own behavior plays in creating their difficulties because they justify non compliance ... are often resistive

and avoidant; frequently blame, deny, and accuse others; either shut down or become highly escalated when they experience strong feelings; create upset and distress in the people around them; are often seen as "difficult" or "bad" rather than psychologically dysfunctional (Lester 3-5).

THEORIES CAUSES
OF PERSONALITY DISORDERS

Psychoanalytic Theory. Cause: Distortions in the early development of the child involving disruption in attachment resulting in the reliance on a very few, very primitive psychological defenses. Problems with psycho-analytic theory: (1) Questionable Validity – Theory based; not data based. (2) Early experience is not reliably predictive because 80% of those who were sexually abused do not develop a personality disorder. There is only a .27 correlation between sexual abuse and Borderline Personality Disorder. One third show no childhood trauma; one third show mild trauma, and one fourth show severe trauma.

Genetic Theory: Cause: direct hereditary transmission of the disorder caused by specific DNA formation. Problems with genetic theory: (1) Even identical twins do not have 100% concordance. Schizotypal twin study showed concordance rates of 4% in fraternal and 33% in identical twins. (2) No reliable genetic markers found yet.

Biosocial Theory: Cause: Personality Disorders are a combination of character (psychological) factors and temperament (biological predisposition) factors. Problems with biosocial theory: (1) Question of how much is biological, how much is environmental is unresolved. (2) A "We don't know, so throw everything in" theory.

It is well established that the "frontal lobes play a crucial role in the regulation of behavior." Dr. Hare points out that "several investigators have argued persuasively that some sort of frontal-lobe dysfunction--not necessarily involving actual damage--may underlie the psychopath's impulsivity and frequent failure to inhibit inappropriate behavior (Hare 169)." Hare concludes that he can "find no convincing evidence that psychopathy is the direct result of early social or environmental factors" and that although "societal factors and parenting practices help to shape the behavioral expression of the disorder" they are not the sole or primary cause of it (Hare 174-178).

A **biological theory** that "has been around for a long time is that, for reasons unknown, some of the psychopath's brain structures mature at an abnormally slow rate. " There is a twofold similarity between an adult psychopath's brain waves and that of normal adolescents and children and a similarity in characteristics such as "egocentricity, impulsivity, selfishness, and unwillingness to delay gratification." Robert Kegan's 1986 research "suggests that psychopathy reflects little more than a developmental delay" and that behind Cleckley's "Mask of Insanity" lies not "insanity but a young child of nine or ten" (Hare 168-169).

Current Prevailing Theory: Presdisposing biology combines with early psychology to create functional biology. Cause: Biological predisposition combines with disruptive early experience(s) to create disorder that then becomes permanent brainwiring. PET scan studies of developing brains accounts for chronicity, early onset, lack of insight, and the different nature of the disorders (Lester 14-15).

TREATMENTS

Dr. Len Sperry feels that a paradigm shift is occurring within the medical profession regarding the prospects for successful treatment of personality disorders by therapists, who, in general, when referred a personality disorder as a client, will tend to feel "stuck, apprehensive or angry." Moreover, most therapists begin to worry about their "personal safety, after hours emergencies, or telephone calls, or whether [their] bill will be paid" (Sperry 1). These are still legitimate concerns when treating personality disorders; however, feelings of futility and hopelessness are beginning to diminish due to expanded approaches to treatment.

Before 1980, personality disorders were mostly conceptualized in terms of "character language." Psychoanalysis and psychotherapy were considered the treatment of choice with the goal of treatment to "change character structure." Today, treatments tend to be more "focused and structured, with the clinician taking a more active role," thus, broadening the approach to include treating character and temperament. Moreover, "neurobiological and biosocial formulations" of personality disorders have also attracted attention and research. Until recently, the "consensus among clinicians was medication did not and could not treat personality disorders per se, but could be used to ... target symptoms such as insomnia" (Sperry 4-6).

Now, low dose antipsychotics are useful for cogni-tive and perceptual problems; serotonin blockers are use-ful for impulsivity and aggression in borderline and anti-social personalities; and antidepressants and serotonin blockers are useful for the avoidant personality type. In general, therapists feel that the "lower the level of treatability, the more the combining and integrating of treatment modalities and approaches is needed."(Sperry 7).

MANAGING PERSONALITY DISORDERS

Dr. Lester recommends the following specific suggestions for managing and preventing problems with personality disorders: Make sure that all agreements are clear and specific, and deal promptly with all broken agreements. Use a team approach because teamwork dilutes intensity. Promptly address all upsets, problems, difficulties, or broken agreements. Pick your battles and do not get sidetracked onto irrelevant issues. Set and maintain firm, reasonable, conscious limits and beware of attempts to talk you out of them. Be willing to let go at any time because over-attachment to outcomes creates vulnerability to drama. Stay focused on your purpose. Manage your energy because fatigue is a risk factor for involvement in drama. Be judicious about criticism because personality disorders have a limited ability to respond well to criticism. Resist psychological transfers by not echoing their feelings of anger by getting angry. Take responsibility for your behavior despite provocations. Don't get caught in the need to be right. Be willing to be defined as wrong if it moves forward your purpose. Give attention because signs of attention and importance can help avoid dramas. Seek to diminish the intensity of escalated outbursts. When in doubt, get an outside opinion because it is easy to lose perspective and get caught in drama. Watch out for feelings of "I'm Crazy" because it's a sign that you are caught in a drama. Get outside help. Limit or avoid exceptions to established rules and procedures. Beware of the victim ploy by responding judiciously or carefully without racing to the rescue. Keep your expectations moderate and appropriate. (Lester 103-104).

In managing the **Antisocial** personality disorder, Dr. Lester's set up is to scare them, get them guessing and keep them off balance. The technique is to apply leverage. Very little works if you can't scare them or if you have no leverage.

The way to manage the **Borderline** personality disorder is to reframe their current emotional state as appropriate to the situation. The technique is to teach them appropriate behaviors framed as "the way to handle the source of this upset or difficulty …"

To manage the **Narcissistic**, the setup is to feed them "rightness" by letting them be right until their neediness calms down. The technique is to ask, suggest, recommend, or request (Lester 106).

TIPS FOR DEALING WITH TOXIC PEOPLE

It is important not to play therapist with a personality disorder or toxic person. Avoid deluding yourself into thinking that you can rescue this person by parenting him or her. For resources and further information, please refer to the Works Cited pages in this book. In the meantime:

(1)   Communicate openly and clearly (in writing if necessary) that unacceptable behavior will not be tolerated and that it has definite consequences;

(2)   disassociate from toxic personalities if they continue the harmful or hurtful behavior while refusing to seek help or to help themselves. Isolating toxic people is a powerful tool for getting them to modify

their behavior since they fear abandonment by those they abuse or misuse. Moreover, they loathe anything that looks like personal rejection.

(3)   Be prepared for passive-aggressive behavior or vendictiveness when you reject or refuse to allow toxic personalities to have their way. They are famous for telling lies or half truths designed to defame, sabotage, isolate, or turn others against you. In extreme cases, antisocial or psychopathic personalities may attempt to harm you physically. The key is not to show fear because they feed off of anything that makes them feel as if they have the upper hand. When trying to get a personality disorder out of your life, do not return phone calls, and ignore emails, or attempts to make contact. The old saying "don't feed it and it'll go away" eventually works. Be courageous and fearless by not bowing down to threats of physical violence; they will not expect you to stand up for yourself because they are accustomed to being bullies and

getting their way through threats and intimidation.

If you are dealing with a toxic employee, it means putting them on notice about their behavior and later firing them if they continue to behave irresponsibly or badly. Do this quickly and decisively before the person becomes comfortable and entrenched in bad behavior that leads this individual to believe that he or she can get away with it. Keep in mind that this does not necessarily mean that a toxic person will make permanent behavioral changes. Usually, all that this means is that they will alter their behavior around you to avoid criticism or reprisal.

If you are in an intimate relationship with a toxic person, nothing will work unless you first get to the point where you are willing to stop playing caretaker for those who are unwilling to change their harmful or self-destructive behavior. You must also be willing or able to leave the person and be ready to deal with your own abandonment issues or fear of being alone. It is imperative that you be able to be alone rather than remain in bad company.

If you are dealing with a toxic child, it is essential to institute cause and consequences for inappropriate behavior; get the child into a routine that creates discipline, social responsibility towards self and others; and teach the child to take into consideration the feelings and needs of others (this also works well with adults). Ask the child to "pretend" that other people have feelings too. Pretty soon this pretense will become a habit that automatically generates considerate behavior.

If you are dealing with relatives, it is helpful to let them know that unless they are willing to leave negative behavior outside your door, they are not welcome in your home and do not visit their homes either.

Please note that nothing will work without sticking to your resolve. Make sure that if you tell a toxic person you are going to do something that you follow through; otherwise, you will only affirm that their behavior has no consequences. Thus, there will be no motivation to change.

It is important not to feel sorry for toxic personalities, not to blame yourself, and not to feel guilty when you refuse to give in to their demands or selfish pleas for help or assistance. Dr. Hare warns us to "be aware of who the victim is" because "psychopaths often give the impression that it is they who are suffering and that it is the victims who are to blame for their misery." He cautions one not to "waste your sympathy on them." Moreover, Dr. Hare reminds us to recognize that we are not alone because "everyone is vulnerable to the psychopath, and there is no shame in being victimized (Hare 215-216)."

If you are wondering, "why bother?" or what can be gained out of using the "tough love" approach with toxic personalities, L. R. Hubbard reminds us that:

> "If you were to weed out and disconnect from antisocial personalities you might experience great relief. Similarly, if society were to recognize this personality type as a sick being and isolate them as they do people with smallpox, both social and economic recoveries could occur. Things are not likely to get much better so long as 20% of the population (antisocials) are permitted to dominate and injure the lives and

enterprise of the remaining 80%. The majority of the population would become sane without interference and destruction from the socially unwell. An understanding and ability to recognize antisocial personalities could bring a major change in society and our lives."

Madonna reminds us that "Freedom comes when you learn to let go. Creation comes when you learn to say no ... There's no greater power than the power of goodbye."

PART III

AFTER THE STORM

REINVENTING RELATIONSHIPS AND RECOVERING SELF ESTEEM

RESILIENT PERSONALITY TRAITS

Often, we get out of one dysfunctional relationship and jump right back into another one. When this happens, we have either failed to learn the lesson from the previous relationship, failed to set minimum standards, or failed to establish boundaries for ourselves; usually, due to ignorance. Since we live in a violent, dominator society, most of us end up part of the "walking wounded." It is refreshing and revitalizing, however, to run across resilient survivors who are still fully capable of loving. In spite of emotional and/or physical wounds, resilient people magically manage to end up with their hearts intact. Unfortunately, the same cannot be said for the majority of the walking wounded, who are incapable of fully loving themselves, which makes it impossible for toxic people to truly love anyone else.

The following traits and characteristics, adapted from Gina O'Connell Higgins' book "Resilient Adults-Overcoming a Cruel Past," help one to size up a potential mate, friend, or business associate, in terms of mental and emotional toughness, or the ability to handle an authentic, peaceful, and loving relationship.

Resilience is defined as the ability to love, along with unusually high levels of functioning in the face of adversity (Higgins 19). Even though toxic personalities may have encountered the same or similar adverse circumstances in life, the resilient person is able to learn from the experience and overcome it. On the other hand, the toxic person has great difficulty learning from experience. He or she fails to take responsibility for his or her actions or reactions, and often becomes embittered by circumstances, vindictive, or worse-for-wear after an encounter with adversity or disappointment, even when at fault. Adult loving is the least expected outcome of a hateful past, yet resilient adults are able to love fully. Toxic people are not (Higgins 23).

Resilient Adults are most repeatedly characterized and described in studies as follows: Above average intellectual competence, cognitive flexibility, information seeking, reflective planning, good school performance, positive appraisal of school experiences, internal locus of control (i.e.

self-control), rational competence with individuals and extended support systems, voluntary and/or mandatory helpfulness in childhood and adolescence, high self esteem, good impulse control, and possession of special talents and inner resources (Higgins 22). In addition, resilient adults also possess the following traits. They:

- Are committed to a measured perspective on the poisonous aspects of the past (believes he or she is the agent of his or her own happiness and is determined not to be subordinated to his or her own suffering);
- Are resolved not to repeat their parents' folly;
- Draw a firm distinction between understanding abusive adults and forgiving them. Holds abusive adults (i.e. parents) fully accountable for their abusive treatment. Believes that reflexively forgiving unrepentant, abusive parents would lead to self betrayal if the parents do not ask for forgiveness or acknowledge the damage and pain they have caused. For that reason, the resilient adult does not love the

abusive parents, yet does not hate them intensely, but rather, feels sorry and ashamed for them ... sees such parents as infantile and primitive.

- Are highly skilled at conflict resolution.
- Are dedicated to maintaining emotional clarity with others.
- Believe they deserve to be loved.
- Are marked by a fundamental decency, integrity, and ingenuousness amidst great sophistication.
- Tend to be preoccupied by their own faults and resist being labeled angel like and saintly. All of them acknowledge their many human shortcomings.

Some resilient traits may be somewhat inborn, but many of them can be learned and thus promoted. In any case, these are the bricks and mortar of overcoming: All of these characteristics are startling when we recall that the resilient came of age stalked by winter's heavy footsteps. These strengths are more remarkable because these people were raised in hell. The resilient are probably kinder and more decent than others, yet they have far more reason to be cruel than most people (Higgins 21-22). The toxic person is cruel without remorse.

REINVENTING RELATIONSHIPS THROUGH SACRED SEX

The Mars Venus split between men and women is at the core of our unhappiness and dissatisfaction in intimate relationships. What we long for is real intimacy, which can only be experienced though sacred sex. It is impossible, however, to bring the sacred into a relationship if you are involved with a toxic personality. It takes the cooperation and commitment of two whole people who are emotionally mature; and, who have healthy attitudes about sex, for a relationship to work. Toxic personalities are emotional infants who cannot behave as adults, especially under stress or when challenged. Thus, once you identify a toxic person, the best thing to do is to weed that individual out of your life, or avoid that person all together, so as to create and make room in your life for a healthy relationship with an adult who has a high emotional IQ; not just a high intellectual IQ.

Sacred sex entails moving beyond lust, guilt, selfishness, and shame into bliss without inner conflict. It involves getting in sync and rhythm with your partner on an emotional, spiritual and intellectual level and surrendering to the mystery of making love with ones body and soul while in harmony with the spirit of the other. Kevin Regan explains that "sexual union is ... at the heart of human life ... [it] is an act of profound worship and praise."

Neale Donald Walsh points out that personal gratification has gotten a bad rap through the years, which is the main reason so much guilt is attached to sex. He says: "You are told you are not to use for personal gratification something that is intensely personally gratifying! This obvious contradiction is apparent to you, but you don't know where to go with the conclusion! So you decide that if you feel guilty about how good you feel during and after sex, that will at least make it all right (Walsh 74).

Walsh adds that "guilt is often used by you in your attempt to feel bad about something you feel good about and thus reconcile yourself with God, who you think does not want you to feel good about anything! Isn't it interesting? All through your life you have been made to feel guilty about

THE THINGS YOU WANT MOST. Yet I will tell you this: love, love, love the things you desire – for your love of them draws them to you" (Walsh 75).

GETTING RID OF GUILT

Walsh urges us to "choose sex ... yet do not choose sex instead of love, but as a celebration of it ... You have been taught that it is better to give than to receive. Yet you cannot give what you do not have. This is not about ignoring the needs of others. Yet life should also not have to be about ignoring your own needs. Give yourself abundant pleasure, and you will have abundant pleasure to give others" (Walsh 75).

Riane Eisler, in her book <u>Sacred Pleasure</u> explains why we are resistant to creating a new sexual paradigm. She relates that "the view that sex has a spiritual dimension is so alien to everything we have been taught that it takes most people completely aback."

Along the same lines. Victoria Lee in her book <u>Ecstatic Lovemaking</u> pinpoints the problem with our current sexual paradigm. She states that "most of us in committed, stable relationships settle for predictability, comfort, and companionship because we fear … the exposure of our deepest selves. Yet in our fear of the unknown, within us and between us, we ignore and avoid the very gift that our commitment sets within our reach – true intimacy."

When one worships another as supreme (both sexually and socially), one denies his or her own divinity (i.e., being created in the image of God), thus, creating low self esteem and a deep longing, which the poet Audre Lorde says stems from the fact that "you are the one that you are looking for."

Those who engage in mindless sex with multiple partners, often experience profound emptiness and self loathing, which ends up getting projected back through acts that degrade the self and others.

What appears to be missing, for most of us, is a view of ourselves and others "as sacred souls on a sacred journey" as Neale Donald Walsh describes it. The truth is, the moment of orgasm brings us as close to heaven, as close to nirvana, and as close to another human being as we can possibly get. Regardless of how we might debase the circumstances surrounding sex, our hearts innately recognize the sacredness of sex. This explains why it is so difficult to disassociate ourselves from dysfunctional or abusive sexual relationships that do not honor us or serve our needs.

Naturally, most people fail to understand the obligation we have, both to ourselves and to others, to honor sex as a sacred act. Ultimately, we also fail to cultivate the self discipline to delay gratification and to refrain from engaging in sex with another whom we do not honor and love or who does not honor and love us. When we fail to do this, we objectify that person and lose sight of their sacredness.

Due to cultural, religious and social conditioning, many have been led to believe that they are entitled to objectify others in their quest to fulfill a fleeting, momentary desire or quest for power over someone. The irony is that when the mission is accomplished, the person who has wittingly or unwittingly used another as an object for self gratification, or for a power trip, becomes baf-fled or bewildered when they discover that the other person had his or her heart open during the act and connected it with the communion of the divine between two sacred souls on a sacred path of discovery through sex with another.

Sadly, as a result of the prevalence of moral and spiritual bankruptcy, we cannot automatically assume that the intentions of another are honorable. We must ask, and then listen to our hearts before succumbing to the heat of passion or before giving in to our primal instincts.

On the other hand, the compassionate thing for a person to do, who has engaged in mindless or uncommitted sex with another, is to summon the courage to be totally honest with that person; to admit that he or she acted out of impulse, without integrity, and out of harmony with spirit; then, ask for that person's forgiveness if they dishonored, objectified, or used and then discarded that person. At that point, healing can begin for both parties. Being dishonest about our intent or not stating our intention upfront only encourages the other person to hope for something that is not forthcoming. Later, this will deepen resentment and make it more difficult for that person to forgive the transgressor for having added insult to injury.

Therefore, to prevent potential problems or heartbreak, before engaging in sex, both parties would do well to come to an agreement about what each of them expects from the encounter; otherwise, someone is bound to end up hurt, angry or disappointed. Moreover, to avoid degrading or diminishing another human being, or exploiting them sexually, it is helpful to shift our consciousness surrounding sex to a higher level and elevate sex to the height it was meant to be: The sacred merger of two souls who are committed to the emotional, spiritual, and physical well being of each other, wherein love of God and love of your lover become one. Of course, it is difficult for this to happen if we succumb too quickly to sexual chemistry before finding out if that person is emotionally or physically available to you or is attuned to the sacredness of others.

In Freudian terms, the "Id" is the childish part of our brains. It urges us toward immediate gratification of our needs without examining the consequences of our actions. Just because we have the urge to do something, does not mean that it is wise to act upon that urge, especially if doing so would cause future harm to yourself, to the other party, or to someone that we are currently involved with. Thich Nhat Hahn urges us to be mindful of future harm that might be caused by a sexual liaison. The operative words are self-mastery, discipline, responsi-bility, self love and consideration for others.

Please note before reading further, that I am not advocating any particular action. Moreover, those who have a sense of entitlement to use others, or who adhere to blind religious beliefs, will miss the point entirely. It might serve one, however, to look at the implications and consequences of casual sexual encounters, particularly when entered under false pretenses. For instance, if all one is after is temporary sexual gratification, without real intimacy, theoretically, it would be less costly emotionally and financially to simply masturbate (it's the only safe sex and no one gets hurt or disappointed) or to pay a prostitute. Masturbation is free; on the other hand, prostitution is a transaction of needs: one person gets his or her sexual needs fulfilled through engagement with the another (without real intimacy), while the prostitute gets a financial need met by permitting his or her body to be used as a receptacle for lust without emotional attachment. The point is, through a transaction of needs, between two consenting adults, neither party is led to believe that the encounter has the promise of anything in the future and no one is misled or disappointed, as opposed to deliberately misleading another into believing that the sexual encounter is more than mere gratification of a need, or a desire for a new sexual conquest.

I am not advocating prostitution; however, it seems fitting to point out the obvious. Indeed, rather than use another individual as an object; to pay for casual sex that is meaningless or degrading to another; or to lead another person on to fulfill selfish desires, (any of which can create needless pain and suffering), masturbation seems to be the least harmful choice. After all, sex is a powerful drive that does not have to lead one into debauchery or degradation, yet it often does that very thing when we are driven by guilt, or attached to blind beliefs that do not make sense or that do not serve us.

Anais Nin says that "life shrinks or expands in proportion to ones courage." It seems that it is time to find the courage to change our core beliefs about sex and female sexuality because it takes courage to remove our blinders and see the painful truth we would rather avoid because we do not want to take responsibility for effecting change in our lives. An Hassidic saying reminds us that "when passion burns within you remember that it was given to you for a good purpose." We do not have to turn it into something debase or dirty. Moreover, Victoria Lee believes that "gradually, we are beginning to understand that what we need is to learn to experience the sacred in our daily lives." Daphne Rose Kingma reminds us that it is "through sex we enter the timeless, boundaryless moment. We partake of the one experience above all others in life which allows us the bliss of true union."

Many women feel that they are not alone in their feelings of disillusionment, weariness, and battle fatigue associated with safe-guarding the fragile self esteem, sexual identity, and alleged superiority of men, along with the alleged inferiority of women. Carolyn Heilbrun states that "to worship the totem of superiority is to protect it" (Heilbrun 187). One way that we protect it is through denial of truth.

Much of our discontent in relationships is associated with the shadow side of a society that fears female sexuality. Heilbrun reveals that it is the female's "hunger for dependency and her fear of autonomy" that urges her to be complicit and to support the male's alleged "divine right" to rule over women, thus, causing one sex to be "burdened with the psychic survival of the other." This belief is associated with the fear that "the penis may collapse, crushing the male ego and the marriage in its flaccidity [i.e. limpness] ... Their exposed male organ is in constant danger of mutilation. It is exposed, it can be struck ... this metaphor for weakness is granted to those with absolute cultural strength and power, so that they may have an excuse to exercise their power" (Heilbrun 187-189).

It seems that it is time for us to discover, honor and embrace real power, which means power "with," not power "over" another.

DEVELOPING PERSONAL INTEGRITY

Dishonesty is its own trap; even when you think you're doing it to keep from hurting other people's feelings. Once others discover that you lied, or withheld the truth because you were afraid of reprisal, loss, or of others being too weak to handle it, feelings of betrayal, deception, or distrust come back to haunt you. Dishonesty, in turn, creates needless suffering and pain by destroying the ability to TRUST or to rely on a person's word. More importantly, if we fail to tell others simple truths that might help them get unstuck or figure out why what they are doing doesn't work, then we are doing them a disservice.

Honesty is also a double edged sword that involves not only being honest with others about what you want and need from them, but being upfront about what you expect in return. That is the real meaning behind the saying, "You've got to be cruel to be kind." What makes this difficult to do is the fact that many people are allergic to the truth; for others, the truth is against their religion (especially for "people of the lie"). It literally makes these people physically ill to confront reality; to face the fact that someone sees through them; or that not everyone appreciates or values deception and dishonesty.

Many people prefer denial, delusion, and detachment rather than reality. The title of Michael Moore's television show "The Awful Truth" reveals that most Americans view the truth as an "awful" or painful pill to swallow. In reality, however, speaking our truths, respecting ourselves, respecting others, and living lives of honesty and integrity is a cure for what ails the world. Most people have this concept backwards because they are out of touch with their authentic selves and are attached to fear, illusions and a need to be accepted by others which causes them to conform to the herd mentality. For those who do not conform, Emerson said that "for your non-conformity, the world whips you with its displeasure." No one said it would be easy to be a person of honesty and integrity, but the rewards of self respect and self esteem are well worth the disapproval of others since the flip side of that coin is that, when you sell yourself short, you end up not liking yourself.

In a society that suffers from low levels of self esteem, one of the hardest lessons to learn is how to love ourselves; how to BE love; and how to receive love from others. Love truly is letting go of fear – the fear of not being loved in return or of losing the object of our love.

In actuality, we pay a high emotional price for dishonesty and lack of integrity with ourselves and others, conveniently supported by cultural and religious indoctrination that views humans as inherently bad, rather than intrinsically good; thus, justifying the inclination toward dishonesty and lack of integrity. If that was the case, then we would not innately attempt to minimize the danger we pose to ourselves and others by seeking punishment (i.e., allowing ourselves to get caught), justifying our bad behavior (e.g., blaming others), or by punishing ourselves. In effect, we possess internal control mechanisms that attempt to prevent us from doing continued harm to ourselves and others. Of course, there are those who condition themselves to override this instinct. Moreover, the problem is heightened by the fact that we are conditioned to distrust intuition, to set aside our instincts, and to cater to low or base desires.

The Catch-22 is that when a person openly transgresses, goes against, or fails to live up to a moral code that an individual has agreed upon as a social norm, this act which will automatically compel him/her to seek a remedy for the situation, be it a good or bad one. Unfortunately, most attempts to resolve this situation are misguided. Keep in mind that since social norms and moral codes vary from culture to culture, and from individual to individual, it can be a costly mistake to assume that others automatically value or adhere to our same moral code or social norm. One would be wise to ask first, just to be sure that he or she is on the same page, in terms of values and expectations.

When a person knowingly or deliberately violates a moral code, then covers up the deed, or fails to disclose the truth for fear of consequences, this non-disclosure will eventually lead to a disintegration of the group, or the relationship.

Once the internal guilt of not coming clean and admitting the wrong against another, or society, becomes too great, the person will make less of the individual or group he or she has wronged in an effort to lessen the emotional burden or to level the playing field. At this point, the person will begin to justify the behavior or make excuses for it. Ultimately, a conflict occurs between the wrong action and the person's innate need to be right; often propelling the person to continue to commit the wrong action over and over again. Of course, this choice creates repetitive behavior with a built-in, downward spiral leading to self-destruction.

Once a person accumulates enough wrongs and/or non-disclosures against another person, or a group, he or she will become critical and begin to find fault with others, or the group, in a deliberate attempt to justify leaving the relationship or the group. Often, the person who commits the wrong will demand to be punished, which can be easily accomplished by the offender pushing the injured party into a corner or into a position of self defense when, in fact, the injured party has done nothing wrong. For example, the wrongdoer may start an argument, slight the person, or strike the other person first, thereby forcing the injured party to fight back, reject that person, or seek revenge. This action creates a reaction that ends up making the injured party punish him or her so that the offender will not feel so alone, guilty, or wrong.

The question that naturally arises is: what can be done to break this non-constructive cycle? The good news is that there is a way to free ourselves from this cycle of stupidity created by doing the same dumb thing over and over again while expecting different results.

For example, TWELVE STEP PROGRAMS advocate going to the person you have wronged, admitting what you've done, then asking for forgiveness, unless to do so would cause greater harm to that person. The point to keep in mind is to take total responsibility for changing the offensive behavior so as not to repeat it. Naturally, this process does not include the practice of going to confession and asking for forgiveness on Sunday, only to repeat the transgression during the rest of the week without bothering to change the behavior.

When it is not possible to go to the individual that you have wronged or harmed, there is another practical solution widely used by therapists and metaphysicians. In fact, L. Ron Hubbard's little booklet "Honesty and Integrity" examines this process in detail. Hubbard encourages us to write down the exact details of the non-disclosure or injury (emotional or physical), being careful to be as specific as possible regarding the details surrounding the event or occurrence. He suggests that one write down each act separately until the individual has written up every single one that he or she can remember committing against anyone or anything as far back as childhood. Then, ask someone you trust to read what you have written, without commenting on the material. The reader is only to acknowledge that he or she has read it.

Writing down this information allows us to cleanse our conscience, admit guilt, and accept responsibility for having transgressed, injured, or wronged another, thereby lifting the burden of guilt created by this offense. Hubbard contends that letting go of guilty feelings allows us to reconnect with our authentic selves and to find renewed self respect. There is a part of us that inherently knows and values truth and integrity. Hubbard feels that our failure to discover truth, or to adhere to it is what gets us stuck in stupid, repetitive, or just plain old insane behavior. Thus, writing down our misdeeds and having someone read them, allows us to move out of the past, where we hate ourselves for things we have done, and into the present where we can forgive ourselves, let go of the past, and embrace the good that is inside of us just waiting to come forth.

NOTE: For more details, refer to L. Ron Hubbard's booklet "Honesty and Integrity."

FORGIVING AND LOVING YOURSELF

FORGIVENESS is the key to letting go of our negative self-image and the burden of self-loathing and fear that too many of us carry around. Forgiveness also unlocks the door to love. Love is what it's all about. Most of us make the mistake of looking for love first and foremost, outside of ourselves, without falling in love with ourselves first. I do not mean in the Narcissistic sense of believing that we are too good for anyone else, but in the practical sense of transforming ourselves into someone who is, first and foremost, capable of loving self unconditionally. Only then will we be able to set and maintain healthy boundaries that will prevent us from allowing others to take advantage of us. At the same time, one would also want to cultivate becoming someone whom others can turn to and find peace, acceptance, kindness, encouragement and unconditional love. In other words, if we want more love in our lives, we have to become move loving to ourselves and be willing to give out more love to others. When we do that, others will naturally come back for more and will automatically want to spend more time with us because we make them feel good about themselves when they are around us, or because we inspire them to experience new possibilities that they, too, can cultivate within themselves.

Holding in resentment, anger, pain, or fear creates dis-ease. Our hearts and bodies cannot heal until we forgive others, but we must first forgive ourselves. Ironically, we tend to find it easier to forgive others than to forgive ourselves. That's because we feel stupid for being gullible or for letting others take advantage of us. What we forget is that our willingness to extend trust to those who pretend to be trustworthy does not reflect badly on us; the fact that our trust was abused reflects badly on the abuser.

In reality, love really is "letting go of fear" since love and fear cannot coexist together. Thus, we have to give up the need to be right, to blame or to hold on to resentment because those feelings are fear based and cannot coexist along side love. We also have to give up our belief in scarcity and learn to trust in the abundance in the universe and tap into it through prayer and meditation. As long as we believe that we cannot replace a lost lover, job, or prized possession, we will hold on, against our best interest, even when it's time to move on, or when we've outgrown the person, job, or possession.

Don Henley, in his song "The Heart of the Matter" (Geffen Records) says that he thinks it's all about:

FORGIVENESS, FORGIVENESS ... Even if, even if, you don't love me anymore ... These times are so uncertain, there's a yearning undefined/And people filled with rage. We all need a little tenderness/How can love survive in such a graceless age?/The trust and self assurance that lead to happiness/They're the very things we kill, I guess...There are people in your life who've come and gone/They'll let you down, you know they'll hurt your pride /You'd better put it all behind you baby cause life goes on/You keep carrying that anger, it'll eat you up inside, baby.

THE PURPOSE OF RELATIONSHIPS
(The following is excerpted and adapted from
"Conversations With God" –Book 2
by Neale Donald Walsh) - Audiotape

The purpose of relationships is to decide what part of yourself you want to have show up, not what part of another you can capture and hold. The purpose of a relationship is to have another whom you might share your completeness -- not to find someone who will complete you. You have no need for a particular other to experience who you really are. It is not true that without a relationship you are nothing. Each person in a relationship should worry about self, not the other person. If we did that then all relationships would serve their purpose. Your focus on the other and your obsession with the other is what causes relationships to fail. It doesn't matter what the other is doing or being; it only matters what you are being in relationship to that.

The most loving person is the person who is balanced or centered within the self. Many seek love of self through love of another. They think that if someone loves them, then they can love themselves because only then are they lovable. This is a sickness. People who do not love themselves embark upon a campaign to have you prove your love and alter your behavior. If you can get them to believe that you love them then they start worrying about how to hold on to you. That's when they begin altering their behavior and losing themselves. That is also when you lose your dignity.

The whole cannot be greater than the sum of the parts. You become less than in such relationships when you give up most of what you are in order to be and stay in relationships.

When you lose sight of each other as sacred souls on a sacred journey, you lose sight of your purpose, which is to evolve and to become. Relationships help you decide what you are becoming. Relationships are holy ground. Blessed are the balanced and the centered for they shall know God. Get to know the highest part of yourself and stay centered in that.

It is necessary for you to first see yourself as worthy, blessed, and to know yourself to be holy before you can acknowledge holiness in others. If you acknowledge another as holy before you acknowledge yourself, you will resent it. One thing we cannot tolerate is someone who is holier than thou. Eventually, we crucify those that we think are holier than thou. You are as holy as am I. All of the great teachers have taught that.

You can never truly fall in love with another until you have truly fallen in love with yourself. It is not in the action of another, but in your reaction, that your salvation will be found.

We should admit to another how we are feeling. This is difficult for many to do. You must honor your feelings, which means honoring yourself, and you must love your neighbor as you love yourself. If you cannot honor the feelings within yourself, how can you honor another? Having your negative feelings or owning them is the only way you can disown those feelings as how you do not want to be.

We should ask: What is the highest choice? Not, what is the most profitable choice, or how can I lose the least? Winning or losing is not the test, only loving or failing to love is the test. A life lived from the level of damage control is a life lived with fear, which speaks a lie about you because you are love, not fear. The only question is "What would love do now?" No other question is relevant, nor has any meaning to your soul.

If you look to what is best for you when you are being abused, at the very least, you will stop the abuse and that will be good for both you and your abuser, for even an abuser is abused when his abuse is allowed to continue. This is not healing to the abuser but is damaging. If the abuser finds that his abuse is acceptable, what has he learned? If the abuser finds that his abuse will be accepted no more, what has he been allowed to discover? Treating others with love does not necessarily mean allowing others to do what they wish. Parents learn this with children. Love cannot work through dishonesty, denial, fear, or people pleasing. Wickedness cannot be allowed to flourish but must be stopped. Love of self and love of the wicked demands it.

DO RELATIONSHIPS CARRY OBLIGATIONS?

You don't have to be the long suffering wife, or the belittled husband, or a victim of your relationship. You don't have to put up with attacks to your dignity, assaults on your pride, damage to your psyche, or wounds to your heart in order to say that you did your best in the relationship, did your duty, or met your obligations in the eyes of God and man.

You have no obligations in a relationship. Never do anything out of a sense of obligation. If you are in the business of creating yourself, as opposed to what someone else wants you to be, it's easy to see that there are no restrictions, limitations, guidelines or rules – nor are you bound by any codes or laws because love is the only law, and love does not bind us, it creates opportunity. Opportunity, not obligation is what relationships offer us.

Be perfectly honest in relationships. Speak your truths kindly and change your truths easily and quickly when you have new clarity. On a conscious level, agree on purpose with your mate. What needs or sets of needs are you trying to fulfill in a relationship? We tend to enter into a transaction of needs. We don't say "I trade you very much," we say "I love you very much."

LONGEVITY IN RELATIONSHIPS

We make it seem as if holding on to a relationship makes it a success. Do not confuse longevity in a relationship with a job well done. Your job is not to see how long you can stay in a relationship; it's to decide and experience who you really are. Love makes no demands, has no expectations.

BECOMING CENTERED IN YOURSELF

The highest choice is that which produces the highest good for you. The highest good for you becomes the highest good for another. What you do for yourself, you do for another. What you do for another, you do for the self since you and the other are one. When you do what you think is best for the other person in the relationship, this only produces continued abuse and continued dysfunction in the relationship. The long-suffering person becomes resentful, angry and distrustful, even of God. Doing what is best for you in the highest sense will not put you in a situation where you will commit an ungodly act because if you love yourself you will not do anything to harm yourself or another.

THE WRONG REASONS TO ENTER INTO A RELATIONSHIP

to end loneliness; to fill a gap;
to bring love; to have someone to love;
to salve one's ego; to end depression;
to improve one's sex life;
to recover from a previous relationship;
or, to ease boredom.
None of the foregoing reasons work.

THE RIGHT REASONS TO ENTER INTO A RELATIONSHIP

To create an opportunity for growth, full self-expression, for lifting your life to its highest potential, for healing every false thought or small idea you have about you, and for ultimate reunion with god through the communion of two souls. If you take those vows, the relationship will get off on a good foot. There are no guarantees. If you want guarantees, then you don't want life, you want a rehearsal. Life cannot have guarantees else its purpose is thwarted.

If other people know that you see them as more, they will show you more. We should give people permission to let go of every false thought they have ever had about themselves. The work of the soul is to wake yourself up. People tend to see in themselves what we see in them. Remind people of who they are and remember who you are. Demonstrating this consistently ultimately reminds others of who they are for they will see themselves in you.

I. Vanzant says that "Total self acceptance, honest acknowledgment, trusting support, and honoring of self is all we need to make a relationship a good one. "

SIX MISTAKES
TO AVOID IN RELATIONSHIPS

Dr. Barbara DeAngelis, in her book "Secrets About Men Every Woman Should Know" gave some truly pragmatic and helpful relationship advice. She recommends that we avoid:

1. Acting like a parent and treating your partner like a child.
2. Sacrificing who you are and putting yourself second in importance to your partner or anyone else.
3. Falling in love with a person's potential.
4. Covering your excellence and competence to allow your loved one to shine or not feel threatened.
5. Giving up your power.
6. Acting like a "macho man" or a "little girl" to get what you want from the opposite sex.

THE NEGATIVE EFFECTS
OF PARENTING AN ADULT

Dr. DeAngelis warns that when you treat an adult like a child, this person will feel judged and criticized, which lowers an individual's self esteem, leading that person to behave incompetently, to resent you, and to rebel against you. Remember, when a person does not feel good about himself or herself, that person will become less loving toward you, which is the quickest way to kill the passion in a relationship.

HOW TO TELL
IF YOU ARE A RESCUE-HOLIC

Dr. DeAngelis also offers simple ways to determine if you're a rescue-holic. Do you tend to do the following:

1. Tell yourself that your partner just needs a little more time to get him/herself and his/her life together, and doing this every few months.
2. Tell yourself that no one has ever really loved your partner enough, and that you will be the one to love him/her enough to change him/her.
3. Feel that everyone else misunderstands your partner - that only you know the "real" person inside of him/her – "You don't know him/her like I do."
4. Make excuses to your friends and family about why your partner either isn't treating you well

or isn't doing well him/herself.

5. Feel that you can't give up on this person and leave him/her, because it will just validate his/her feelings of worthlessness, and then he/she will never change.

6. Convince yourself that, even though your partner doesn't give you that piece of him/herself and his/her heart, what he/she does give you makes it worth staying in the relationship.

HEALING OLD
RELATIONSHIP PATTERNS

Before becoming involved in a new relationship, or dissolving a current one, examine what type of fear games you are playing with each other. This examination can help you avoid repeating old patterns in new relationships.

FEAR GAMES:

There are three common fear patterns that Jan Kennedy outlines in her book "The Venus Factor – 7 Steps to a Loving Relationship".

Parent & Child – The emotional fear game wherein we create the same kind of emotional dependency needs we experienced as children. What you end up with is another frightened child looking for the same thing that we are – one who is willing to team up with us to create the illusion of a nurturing, protective relationship.

In actuality, there never really is a parent – only two fearful children. When we take on the parent role, we have less faith in a benevolent universe than the child we are playing with. At least the child believes there is a mommy and daddy. As a parent figure, we have no one to fall back on but ourselves. Our capacity to experience and share emotional nurturance is directly related to our capacity to trust.

Dealer & Addict – The Physical Fear Game wherein we associate physical pleasures with people or objects instead of recognizing that the capacity for experiencing and sharing physical pleasure resides within yourself.

Once we have projected this power outside of ourselves, we are put in the position of having to maintain the availability of that pleasure.

The dealer's role is to withhold what the addict wants until proper payment is rendered or until the person behaves. To be the dealer you must be the one who is desired and needed. The dealer must shield himself from desiring the addict or he loses control. Thus, he has to indulge himself in pain. This game requires jealousy and revenge. "If you don't want it maybe someone else does!"

The addict's role is to find out what it is the Dealer wants in exchange and then offer it to him. The role of the addict is uncontrolled payment. "Anything you want is yours. Just ask." If one is afraid of losing someone or something, it isn't really theirs. What one is losing is the illusion of having had that person. Put your energy into positive emotions by not resisting the loss of something that you never really had anyway.

Solution: Recognize that all fears are the result of your inability to believe in a benevolent universe and proceed to trust.

Guru vs. Guru. The Mental Fear Game wherein Guru's ask "Do you know what's wrong with you?" then proceed to point out how imperfect others are and teach them the error of their ways. Free spirits and Disciples don't make good partners for the guru game. Only Gurus can really play the game because they are the only ones who have enough in common to keep the game going.

The only requirement for any relationship game is to find another human being whose emotional fears have driven them to play the same game that we are playing. Sometimes we switch roles, or we have to leave the relationship and find a new partner who is more cooperative.

Solution: Fear is the result of being out of harmony with the universe. Pain, anxiety, and anger cannot sustain themselves in a world of love and trust. Choose peace.

TAKING RESPONSIBILITY
FOR YOUR HAPPINESS

The question we have to ask ourselves is: Are we willing to work for what we want? To be worthy, we have to be willing to give up something. Gertrude Stein said: "I do want to get rich but I never want to do what there is to do to get rich."

In his book, <u>Only Fear Dies,</u> Barry Long states that: "The world is the unhappy superstructure that man has imposed on the earth. The world consists of his problems. The earth is beautiful, joyous, cosmic, eternal, problem free." Long also points out that if we want to embrace happiness, we have to dissolve our attachment to the world and its values, which means learning to live in the eternal now, or the present. After all, the present is a gift and the present time is the only time on earth. Anything we love or become attached to in the world will cause us pain. Our pain and confusion is our love of the world. When we surrender the right to be unhappy in the world we become free on earth. But first, we have to face our fears. (Long 1-3)

EMOTIONAL LIBERATION

Marianne Williamson

Our deepest fear is not that we are inadequate. Our deepest fear is that we are powerful beyond measure. It is our light, not our darkness, that most frightens us. We ask ourselves:

Who am I to be brilliant, gorgeous, talented and fabulous? Actually, who are you not to be? You are a child of God. Your playing small does not serve the world. There is nothing enlightened about shrinking so that other people will not feel insecure around you. You were born to make manifest the glory of God that is within us. It is not just in some of us; it is in everyone.

And as we let our light shine, we unconsciously give other people permission to do the same. As we are liberated from our fear, our presence automatically liberates others.

Note: Also quoted by Nelson Mandela at his inauguration.

HEALING AND RELAXING
SOUND EXERCISES

Try the following mindful and meditative exercises whenever you are feeling stressed to help expel negative emotions from the body. Take a deep breath and do each exercise three times, then note how relaxed and relieved you feel.

The HEART holds RESENTMENT. To release it, open your mouth wide and say "Haaaaaaa," recreating the natural sound of relief or satisfaction.

The LIVER is the seat of ANGER. To release pent up anger, make the sound of "Sheeeeee" (as if you are telling someone to be quiet)

The LUNGS hold in SADNESS. To release sadness, place teeth together to make a hissing "Sssssssssss."

The KIDNEYS hold FEAR. Round your lips into a hollow "O" sound and blow out air to recreate an eerie, ghostly "Oooooo" sound from deep in the chest.

The STOMACH is the seat of ANGUISH or ANXIETY. Make a hawking sound from the back of the roof of your mouth, as if clearing your sinus.

BEING PEACE
By: Thich Nhat Hanh

Do not be idolatrous about or bound to any doctrine, theory, or ideology ... all systems of thought are guiding means; they are not absolute truths. Do not think that the knowledge you presently possess is changeless, absolute truth.

Avoid being narrow-minded and bound to present views. Learn and practice non-attachment from views in order to be open to receive others viewpoints. Truth is found in life and not merely in conceptual knowledge.

Do not criticize or condemn things that you are not sure of. Always speak truthfully and "constructfully." Have the courage to speak out about situations of injustice, even when doing so may threaten your own safety.

Sexual expression should not happen without love and commitment. Sexual relations should be aware of future suffering that may be caused. To preserve the happiness of others, respect the rights and commitments of others.

Be fully aware of the responsibility of bringing new lives into the world. Meditate on the world into which you are bringing new beings.

281

TEN STEPS TO SELF ESTEEM

Adapted from "The Ten Commandments of Self Esteem"
by Catherine Cardinal, PhD

I. Do not hang out with people who make you feel bad about yourself.

II. Stop trying to make sense out of the crazy behavior of others. (There is no logic to illogical behavior).

III. Do not keep company with those who are more dysfunctional than yourself. (Model yourself after someone who has already mastered the type of behavior you are trying to achieve).

IV. Trust your body since your mind will play tricks on you. (Gut feelings are trying to tell you something).

V. Give yourself permission, at all times, to say "no;" to change your mind; and, to express your true feelings.

VI. What is not right for you is also not right for others. (Don't make excuses for others).

VII. Do not give beyond your own capacity. (Doormats get walked on. You'll end up resentful).

VIII. What others think of you is none of your business; therefore, do not waste time seeking approval of others nor worrying about what they think of you.

IX. Wherever you are, that's where the party is.

X. Sing your own praises all the days of your life.

WORKS CITED

Benjamin, Lorna Smith. INTERPERSONAL DIAGNOSIS AND TREATMENT OF PERSONALITY DISORDERS - 2nd Ed. Guilford Press (1996).

Cardinal, Catherine PhD. THE TEN COMMANDMENTS OF SELF ESTEEM.

DeAngelis, Barbara. SECRETS ABOUT MEN EVERY WOMAN SHOULD KNOW.

Dutton, Donald G. THE DOMESTIC ASSAULT OF WOMEN UBC Press:Vancouver (1995).

Eisler, Riane. SACRED PLEASURE. Harper-SanFrancisco (1996).

Hanh, Thich Nhat. ANGER - Wisdom For Cooling The Flames."

Hare, Robert D. Phd. PSYCHOPATHY: Theory and Research. NY:Wiley (1970).

Hare, Robert D. PhD. WITHOUT CONSCIENCE. Guilford (1993)

Higgins, Gina O'Connell. RESILIENT ADULTS-Overcoming a Cruel Past.

Heilbrun, Carolyn. REINVENTING WOMANHOOD. Norton:NY (1979).

Hubbard, L. R. "THE CAUSE OF SUPPRESSION" - Bridge Publications

Hubbard, L. R. "INTEGRITY AND HONESTY" - BridgePublications

Kegan, Robert. "The Child Behind the Mask:Sociopathy as Developmental Delay. In W. H. Reid, D. Dorr, J. I. Walker, and J. W. Bonner, III. UNMASKING THE PSYCHOPATH: NY:W.W.Norton (1986).

LaViolette, Alyce: BATTERED WOMEN, Power and Family Systems Therapy (310)493-1161

Kennedy, Jan. THE VENUS FACTOR - 7 Steps to a Loving Relationship

WORKS CITED (cont.)

Lee, Victoria. ECSTATIC LOVEMAKING-An Intimate Guide to
          Soulful Sex. Weisner(2002).
Lester, Gregory W. PhD PERSONALITY DISORDERS IN
          SOCIAL WORK PRACTICE. Heritage Professional
          Education, L.L.C. (1998). Phone: 303-399-3406
Long, Barry. ONLY FEAR DIES. Barry Long Books. Australia/
          England (1994).
Pines, Maya. "New Focus on Narcissism Offers Insight Into
          Grandiosity and Emptiness," *N. Y. Times, 3/16/82*, p. C-1.
Sanford, Linda T. & Donovan, Mary E. WOMEN AND SELF
          ESTEEM. Penguin:NY 1984.
Sperry, Len M.D. HANDBOOK OF DIAGNOSIS AND
          TREATMENT OF DSM-IV PERSONALITY DISORDERS.
          Brunner/Mazel (1995).
Walsh, Neale Donald "CONVERSATIONS WITH GOD – Book 2"
          Hampton Roads Publishing Company
Marianne Williamson. A RETURN TO LOVE.

BOOKS FOR FURTHER READING

Allen, James – AS A MAN THINKETH

*Ariel Books - BELIEVING IN OURSELVES. Andrews &
        McMeal*

*Baisden, Michael: NEVER SATISFIED- How and Why Men
        Cheat. Legacy Publishing*

*Barnett & LaViolette: IT COULD HAPPEN TO ANYONE- Why
        Battered Women Stay. Sage Publications*

Becker, Gavin de: THE GIFT OF FEAR. Little, Brown

Breathnach, Sarah Ban SIMPLE ABUNDANCE. Warner

*Cardinal, Catherine PhD "The Ten Commandments of
        Self Esteem"*

Carter & Sokol: WHAT SMART WOMEN KNOW. Dell

*Cleckley, Hervey. THE MASK OF SANITY. Emily S. Cleckley,
        Publishers, 3024 Fox Spring Road, Augusta, GA 30903.*

Eisler, Riane. THE CHALICE AND THE BLADE. Harper

Fein & Schneider: THE RULES. Warner Books

*French, Marilyn THE WAR AGAINST WOMEN
        Random House*

Hawker & Bicehouse: END THE PAIN, Barclay House

Hayes, Jody: SMART LOVE

*Hendrix, Harville Ph.D.: KEEPING THE LOVE YOU FIND
        Pocket Books*

Hollander, Dory Ph.D.: 101 LIES MEN TELL WOMEN
        HarperCollins

Huffington, Arianna THE FOURTH INSTINCT - The Call
        of the Soul (A Simon & Schuster Audio Tape)

Lieberman, Carole., M.D. & Cool, Lisa: BAD BOYS

Mother Love: LISTEN UP, GIRLFRIEND
        St. Martin's Press

Prather, Hugh & Gayle: PARABLES FROM OTHER
        PLANETS Bantam Books

BOOKS FOR FURTHER READING
(cont.)

Peck, Scott M.: THE ROAD LESS TRAVELED
      Simon & Schuster
Redfield, James: THE CELESTINE PROPHECY
      Warner Books
Rule, Ann. THE STRANGER BESIDE ME. NY:Signet (1980)
Vanzant, Iyanla ACTS OF FAITH & IN THE MEANTIME
Walker, Alice ANYTHING WE LOVE CAN BE SAVED